HISTORICAL ATLAS OF TRAFFORD

DON BAYLISS

First published in 1996
by Don Bayliss, 51 Chiltern Drive, Hale, Altrincham, Cheshire WA15 9PN.

© Don Bayliss 1996
ISBN 0 9529300 0 5

Typeset by Northern Writers Advisory Services, 77 Marford Crescent, Sale,
Cheshire M33 4DN.

Printed by John Roberts, Printers (Salford) Ltd, 162 Chapel Street, Salford,
Greater Manchester.

CONTENTS

ILLUSTRATIONS

ACKNOWLEDGEMENTS

Help has been gratefully received from the following:

Ian Sandham for many, many hours constructing computerised maps without which the maps in this atlas would not have been so clear, and for a great deal of other assistance;

Norman Redhead for permission to use the facilities of GMAU, and Mike Nevell of UMAU, for help and encouragement;

Norman Dore for his historical expertise, editorial and factual assistance;

Ron Higginbottom for proof reading and suggestions;

Chris Perkins for use of maps in Manchester University Department of Geography;

The Ordnance Survey for permission to use maps;

Andrew Macfarlane of Altrincham Electric Railway Preservation Society for material on railways;

Charles Foster of Arley Hall for details of Warburton;

George Morton, Trafford MBC, for many helpful suggestions on recent developments and for encouragement;

Jayne Britton, Lynn Stephenson and staff of Trafford Local Studies Centre, Sale Library, for help with numerous enquiries and use of records and facilities;

Val Freeman of Altrincham Library;

Cheshire Record Office for tithe maps;

John Hodgson of the University of Manchester Rylands Library;

Staff of Salford local history library;

Frank Prest, formerly of MMU;

Alan Morrison of Ashton and Sale History Society;

Derek Pierce and Pat Faulkner of South Trafford Archaeological Group;

Len King of Urmston History Society;

Bill Ashton of Stretford Local History Society;

and many other acquaintances and friends for odd facts willingly or unwittingly given;

Jill Groves of Northern Writers Advisory Service for much advice, typesetting and helping with publication.

Last but not least my wife Hilda for constant checking and putting me back on the right lines whenever necessary.

INTRODUCTION

This atlas describes the location of features of the landscape, human habitations and activity from prehistoric times to the present in the 110 square kilometres (40 square miles) occupied by Trafford Metropolitan Borough. The author is fascinated by maps and these, both old and new, are used to illustrate the history of the Trafford area in a rather different way from a traditional book. The atlas shows the distributions and patterns of where people lived and their activities and work from times past to the present. For convenience the area considered is referred to as Trafford for all periods even though this term did not apply before 1974 when the Metropolitan Borough was created.

Trafford is fortunate to possess many ancient features which, on maps, make interesting patterns and it is the aim of this atlas to identify some of them and present, as in the inspirational historical atlas of Cheshire, by Sylvester and Nulty,[1] 'a handful of still pictures from the moving kaleidoscope of Time.' The author has selected a number of periods and for each of these a map will be shown and explained by an accompanying description. Limited space has also meant concentration on a selection of places to be described.

Using maps is an alternative and attractive way of looking at the past. Much of the information which is shown on the maps of early times, has been extracted from the 'Sites and Monuments Record' for Trafford produced by the Greater Manchester Archaeological Unit. For readers wanting more detail, the book on *The Archaeology of Trafford*, funded by Trafford MBC and written by UMAU and GMAU gives a more specialised picture.[2]

The cartographic approach, including the interpretation of patterns on maps, cannot tell the whole story but can show the reasons why some features of life were located at particular points and so will cast a new dimension on the history of the area. This involves use of old maps which are sometimes artistically very attractive but can be inaccurate (and in some cases rather indecipherable through their age!). Some recent maps are also used but, though they are reproduced here in monochrome and not in colour, they are still able to reveal their secrets.

Throughout the atlas the modern boundaries, and names, of places in Trafford have been used to create a base-map on which features from different periods are shown.

1 THE LANDSCAPE

The landscape in which events have occurred, Fig. 1, should not be thought of as a fixed stage or backcloth.[3] It has been constantly changing, both naturally and by human hands. What was once a heath (as the name tells us) at Broadheath, shunned by early man for his settlements, became at a later period a site occupied by world famous machine-tool firms. During the Ice Age what had been a hollow under the ice became in less cold times after the Ice Age a hunting ground for Mesolithic man, and subsequently in more temperate times, a large bog – Carrington Moss. As time went on man became more capable of shaping his environment to his needs and Carrington Moss, drained in late Victorian times, became an intensively farmed area. The floodplain of the Mersey is now used for a motorway and water park, a reminder that physical features do not permanently constrain human activities.

The highest land is made by a ridge across the south from Dunham to Hale, which reaches 67 metres (219 feet) above sea-level near Bowdon Church and 66 metres (216 feet) at Hale Barns. This ridge was attractive to early settlement due to its fertile soils and good drainage and its command of the view (for security) over the Mersey plain to the north and the Cheshire plain to the south. It was also attractive in the last century for residential development because of its trees, clear air and views. The lowest point of the Trafford area is at 11 metres (36 feet) near Warburton. Much of the rest of the borough consists of flattish land rising in low sweeps or undulating shallow terraces to the east where it reaches 25 metres (81 feet).

The main natural drainage was by two meandering rivers both liable to flood widely. The Irwell flowed from the north-east and was joined north of Partington by the upper Mersey which flows from the east; they then continued south-westwards as the Mersey, and were canalised as the Manchester Ship Canal. The wide upper Mersey floodplain across the body of Trafford played a significant role as a major frontier and boundary for centuries. In the distant past the land of Trafford was occupied on several occasions by different human groups coming from different directions towards the Mersey. The river was also part of the county boundary between Lancashire and Cheshire for seven centuries. The changing course meant that parts of the land south of the river such as the southern end of Crossford Bridge ended up in Lancashire while part of east Stretford, once in Lancashire became part of Cheshire.[4]

Smaller streams such as the Sinderland and Timperley brooks in the south rise on higher land then flow north-westwards before turning west to join the Mersey. One stream drained from Hale Moss through Altrincham and was powerful enough to support a watermill. Where there were no streams the soils of Trafford presented no difficulty to the digging of wells, necessary when population grew in areas away from streams. An artesian basin underlies Trafford Park, tapped for industrial purposes.

More than two thirds of the boundaries of Trafford lie along water-courses including for the western and northern boundary the Ship Canal which did not come into existence until 1894. Rivers and streams such as the Irwell, Mersey, Bollin, Fairywell Brook, Baguley Brook, Red Brook and Sinderland Brook served for centuries as limits of former townships which were eventually joined in 1974 to make the Metropolitan Borough. The old Roman road Watling Street has been included on the map because it was important in early times, and some modern place-names to help identify locations.

Features unfavourable to early settlement included the peat bogs, moors or mosses.[5] The two largest, Trafford and Carrington mosses, lay in hollows in the flat lands of west Trafford. Composed mainly of sphagnum, the mosses were 'raised bogs' which had grown as domes of peat, some up to 5 metres high, rising above the low plains. Even in the late nineteenth century it was not possible to see across Carrington Moss because of its height. Other areas unfavourable to early man were heaths and moors, such as Urmston Moor and Broadheath; also the wide flooding valleys of the streams were avoided. The Mersey flats, with only a few bridges, are still a barrier today between north and south Trafford.

Fig. 1 SOME EARLY LANDSCAPE FEATURES

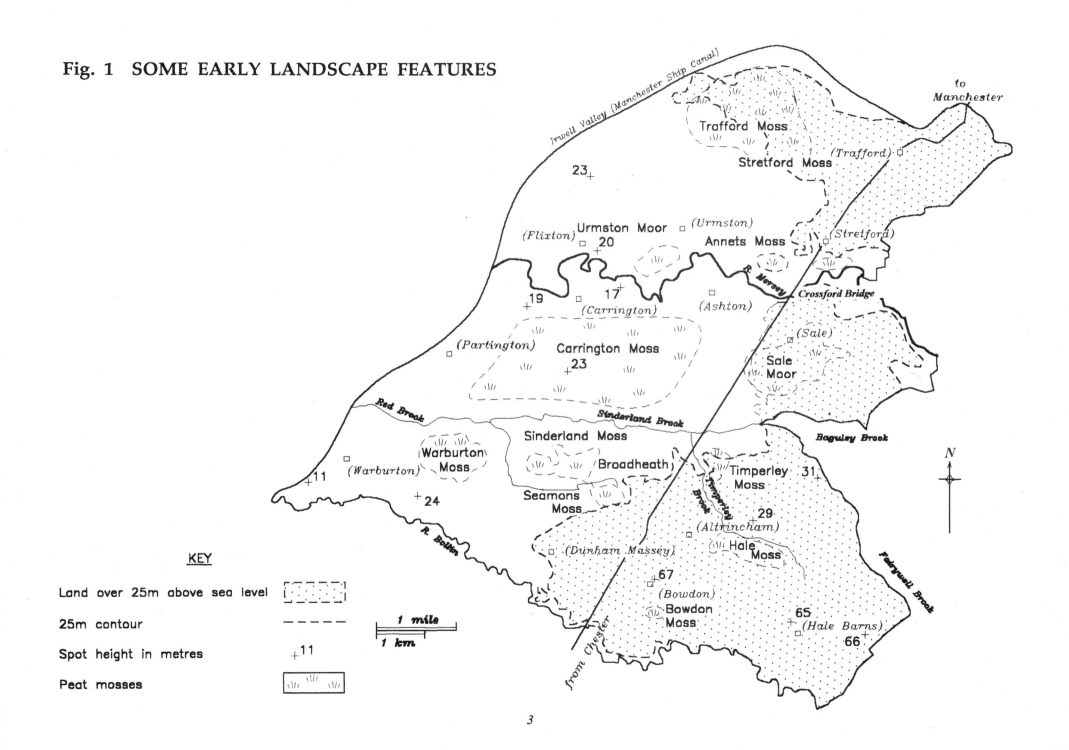

Irwell Valley (Manchester Ship Canal)

to Manchester

Trafford Moss

Stretford Moss

(Trafford)

23 +

Urmston Moor   (Urmston)

(Flixton)   20   Annets Moss   (Stretford)

+ 19   17 +   (Ashton)   R. Mersey   Crossford Bridge

(Carrington)   (Sale)

(Partington)   Carrington Moss   Sale Moor

+ 23

Red Brook   Sinderland Brook   Baguley Brook

Sinderland Moss   N

(Warburton)   Warburton Moss   Broadheath   Timperley Moss   31 +

+ 11   Seamons Moss   29   (Altrincham)   Fairywell Brook

+ 24   R. Bollin   Timperley Brook   Hale Moss

(Dunham Massey)   + 67   (Bowdon)

65 +   (Hale Barns)

Bowdon Moss   66 +

from Chester

KEY

Land over 25m above sea level

25m contour

Spot height in metres   + 11

Peat mosses

1 mile

1 km

2 GEOLOGY, CLIMATE AND VEGETATION

The basement rocks[6] are of Triassic date, for example, sandstones and marls, but these are rarely exposed, except, for example, at Timperley (where they were quarried). They contained important salt brine deposits emerging as springs at Bowdon and Dunham Woodhouses. Because of their limited exposures, the solid rocks are not shown on a map in this atlas. Superficial ('drift') deposits have been far more important to man and dominate the landscape of Trafford, Fig. 2.[7] These derive from the last glaciation, 25-12000BP ('*years before the present*') and to the post-glacial period, from 12000BP onwards. The oldest of the drifts of the last glaciation is a heavy clay-with-boulders laid down under the ice, found in north Hale, Timperley and Old Trafford. Overlying this, glacial sands and gravels which had been carried within the ice were deposited to form the Dunham to Hale ridge (the 'Altrincham ridge'). Much of the rest of Trafford is covered with fluvio-glacial sands deposited when the ice melted. The Shirdley Hill Sand was an aeolian deposit blown in fierce storms after the ice disappeared, and laid down in a blanket creating heaths such as Broadheath. After the Ice Age the rivers began to flow and when they flooded alluvium was deposited, through which terraces were cut.

The 'mosses'[8] first developed from the sphagnum plant which had colonised hollows in the land surface and overwhelmed stretches of post-glacial pine forest in the tundra conditions. The bogs developed in more than one period after 12000BP and covered earlier human settlement as they spread. The chief 'wetlands' were Trafford and Carrington mosses; others were Annets, Bowdon, Hale, Seamons, Sinderland, Stretford, Timperley and Warburton. The mosses dried and shrank naturally and were finally drained by cutting ditches. Broadheath, Sale and Urmston moors were drier heaths.

One particular drift deposit attracted early man: the glacial sands and gravels of the Altrincham ridge on which the natural soils were fairly fertile and carried light woodland. The soils were easy to clear with early tools, were well-drained and yielded a fair return.

The fluvio-glacial sands which cover much of the lower parts of Trafford were also light soils but were damp and early man was only attracted to their drier margins, for example, the string of settlements on either side of the Mersey. Boulder clay provided most potential fertility but the soil was heavy to work and some was not taken into production until medieval times.[9] Moss and alluvial lands were not initially usable for agriculture but could be used for animal grazing in dry seasons. In later times, draining, marling and fertilising created productive agricultural soils from the least promising subsoil.

Climate, vegetation and soils changed many times.[10] A cold period to 10000BP covered the district with tundra. Climate subsequently ameliorated in the Boreal and Atlantic periods from 10000 to 7000BP. At this time, coincident with the Mesolithic (Middle Stone Age), birch, hazel, pine and alder forest covered the land and peat bogs grew. There followed the 'Atlantic' milder, wetter, 'oak-elm' phase from 7000-2500BP culminating in the warm 'Climatic Optimum' (2-3°C warmer than now) enjoyed by Neolithic farmers. After this the Bronze Age was warm and dry but then coolness returned and the mixed forest was replaced by thick alder-birch-oak-ash forest. In the cool and damp 'Sub-Atlantic' period in Iron Age and Roman times, there was a second phase of peat formation. It was warmer in the Dark Ages but deteriorated to the Little Ice Age in the seventeenth and eighteenth centuries.

Human groups also changed the landscape and any new set of invaders would have to adapt to or change the landscape inherited from the previous culture. From Neolithic times onwards there was a steady depletion of woodland to make way for farming. In times of population increase, more land would be cleared and cultivated. In times of population decline (for example, after the Black Death of 1348) farmland would revert to woodland. The landscape was always in flux.

Fig. 2 GEOLOGY – DRIFT DEPOSITS

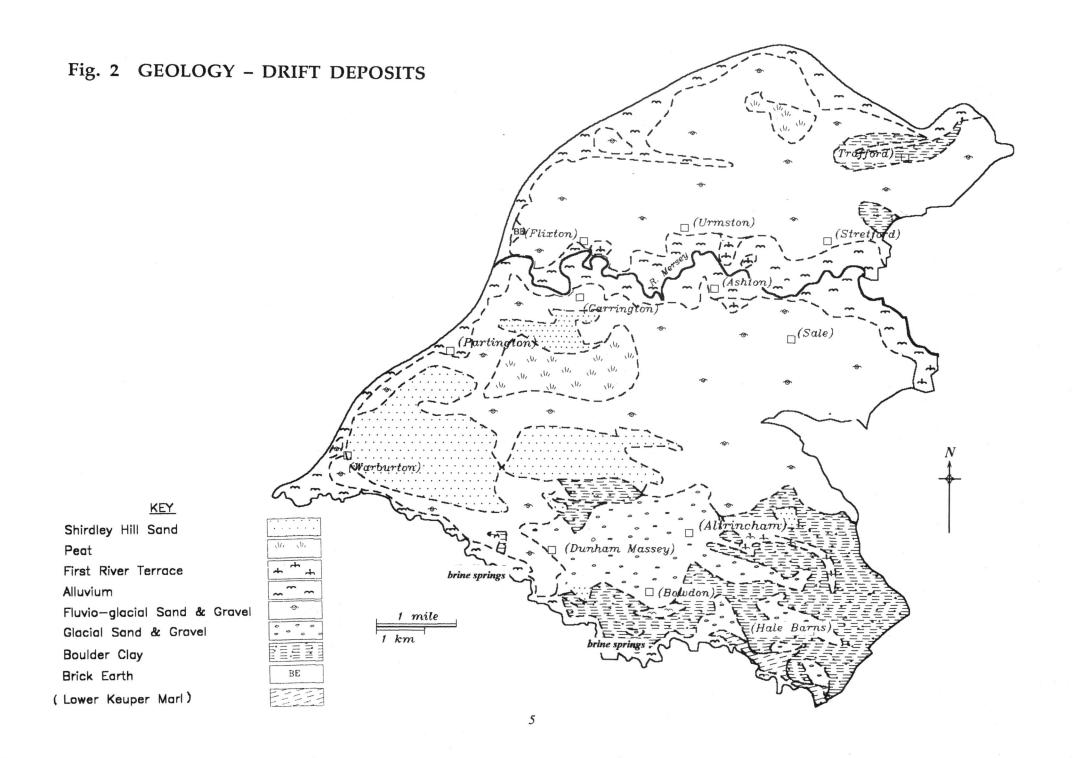

KEY

Shirdley Hill Sand	
Peat	
First River Terrace	
Alluvium	
Fluvio–glacial Sand & Gravel	
Glacial Sand & Gravel	
Boulder Clay	
Brick Earth	BE
(Lower Keuper Marl)	

N

1 mile

1 km

(Trafford)

(Urmston)   (Stretford)

BE (Flixton)

(Ashton)

(Carrington)

(Sale)

(Partington)

(Warburton)

(Altrincham)

(Dunham Massey)

brine springs

(Bowdon)

brine springs

(Hale Barns)

R. Mersey

3 PREHISTORIC AND ROMAN TIMES

The earliest evidence of man in Trafford, **Fig. 3**[11] includes finds of flint arrowheads of the Neolithic period (4500-3800BP)[12] at Altrincham, Dunham and Sale, flints at Timperley Old Hall site, a scraper at Altrincham and stone axes at Flixton and Stretford. It is likely the flint was traded from Northern Ireland. The axes may have been used for felling forest which covered the land to make room for corn agriculture.

The Bronze Age followed (3800-2500BP) but some stone tools continued to be used. The finds of perforated axe-hammers at Timperley and Stretford suggest forest clearance was continuing. The Timperley find was on boulder clay, which in the dry and warm conditions at the time would have been covered in open oak forest. Several prehistoric finds on or near to the Altrincham ridge or close to the (later) Roman Watling Street, suggest there might have been a pre-Roman route from north-east to south-west between the mosses along the eastern side of Trafford. Bronze Age sites are found on slightly higher ground. There are burial mounds signifying some settlement nearby at Hale Low,[13] at Urmston and Warburton and a 'circular feature' of this date at Hooley Hill near Dunham.

In the Iron Age (from 2500BP and through Roman times), Higham[14] suggests Celtic peoples of two different tribes inhabited Trafford, separated by the Mersey valley which served as a frontier. North of the Mersey the Brigantian tribes had entered the area from the north, whilst south of the Mersey lived the Cornovii based at Wroxeter. Enclosures possibly from this period were sited on the Shirdley Hill Sand between Dunham and Carrington Moss, and in the Urmston area on a bluff overlooking the Mersey. There are no defensive works between these two peoples. Two stone heads in Sale possibly may show the Celtic practice of head worship.[15] Several such heads have been found in north-west England. There seems to be an association between prehistoric finds and sites with the higher or better drained soil areas.

The Romans entered the area about AD70 and left about AD410. Mamucium (Manchester), a mile north of the Trafford boundary, was a fort and civil settlement.[16] Trafford was in Mamucium's sphere of influence, crossed by the road from Chester to York (Watling Street) close to which were finds of Roman coins in Bowdon, amphora handles, other fragments of pottery in West Timperley, pottery in Urmston, Davyhulme and Old Trafford, a Roman-British coin hoard in Sale and Roman urn stoppers in Stretford. Another alignment of sites and finds crosses the south of the Borough. A Romano-British settlement may have existed in Hale Barns.[17] It is believed the line of the A538 through Hale Barns was a Roman road;[18] which might have extended to Warburton, this assumption being reinforced by the find of 'beehive'-shaped querns there in 1995.[19]

Prehistoric distributions contrasted with the Roman and Romano-British. The former formed clustered patterns in south Trafford from Altrincham to Warburton and in the Mersey valley and Sale. The latter were mainly in two linear patterns from Hale to Bowdon and along Watling Street and in isolated places in the Stretford and Urmston area. There is no Roman evidence from two districts which previously had prehistoric settlement, Timperley and east Sale, although a coin hoard in west Sale may represent an attempt at settlement.[20] The pattern suggests a limited Roman influence possibly because the area had partly reverted to dense forest in the wet Iron Age.

One feature contradicts this minimalist scenario, the unusual rectangular alignment of modern roads in Trafford, **Fig. 3a**. Research in parts of Manchester has suggested land in Roman times was laid out in rectangular fields (to feed Mamucium) by a process called 'centuriation'[21] resulting in a lattice pattern of roads. The evidence from the inset modern map shows that several present routes may run along alignments of roads planned by the Romans making a grid pattern laid out at right angles to Watling Street suggesting a greater Roman presence than hitherto considered.

Fig. 3 PREHISTORIC AND ROMAN SITES AND FINDS

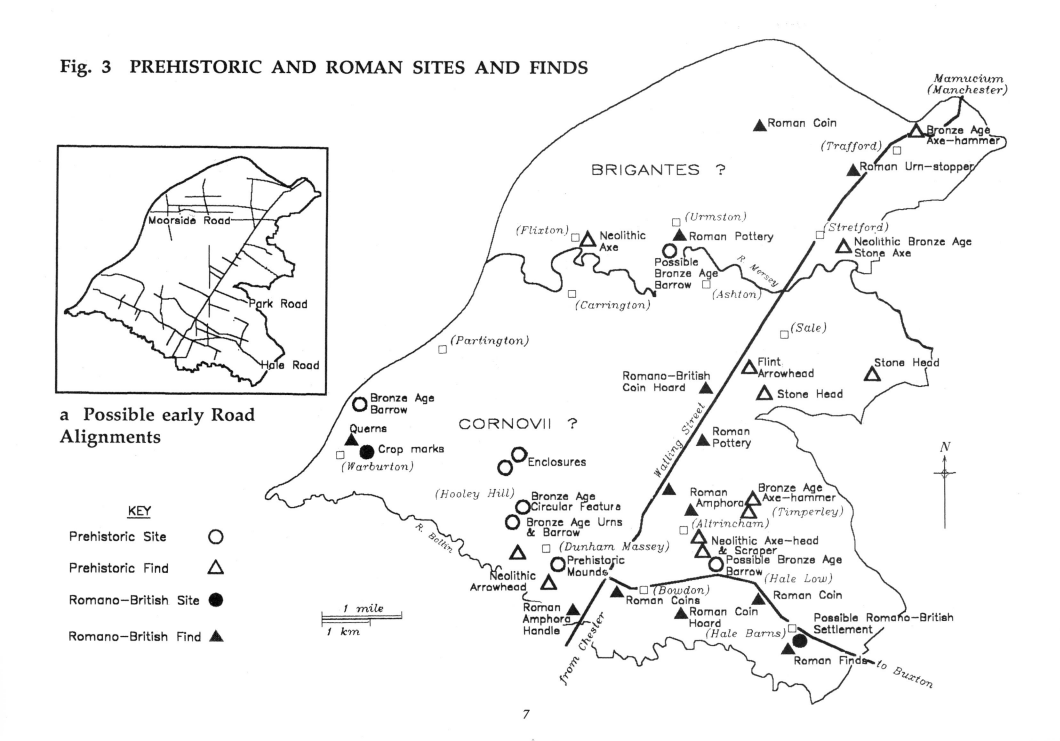

a Possible early Road Alignments

Moorside Road

Park Road

Hale Road

KEY

Prehistoric Site ○

Prehistoric Find △

Romano-British Site ●

Romano-British Find ▲

Mamucium (Manchester)

▲ Roman Coin

Bronze Age Axe-hammer

(Trafford)

BRIGANTES ?

▲ Roman Urn-stopper

□ *(Urmston)*

(Stretford)

(Flixton) △ Neolithic Axe

▲ Roman Pottery

△ Neolithic Bronze Age Stone Axe

○ Possible Bronze Age Barrow

R. Mersey

□ *(Carrington)*

(Ashton)

□ *(Sale)*

(Partington) □

△ Flint Arrowhead

Stone Head △

Romano-British Coin Hoard ▲

△ Stone Head

○ Bronze Age Barrow

CORNOVII ?

Roman Pottery ▲

Watling Street

Quern ▲

□ ● Crop marks

(Warburton)

○○ Enclosures

(Hooley Hill)

○ Bronze Age Circular Feature

▲ Roman Amphora

Bronze Age Axe-hammer △

△

(Timperley)

○ Bronze Age Urns & Barrow

□ *(Altrincham)*

R. Bollin

△ △ Neolithic Axe-head & Scraper

△ △

○ Possible Bronze Age Barrow

(Hale Low)

△ *(Dunham Massey)* □

○ Prehistoric Mounds

△ Neolithic Arrowhead

▲ Roman Coin

□ *(Bowdon)*

▲ Roman Coins

▲ Roman Amphora Handle

from Chester

▲ Roman Coin Hoard

(Hale Barns)

□ Possible Romano-British Settlement

●

▲ Roman Finds *to Buxton*

1 mile

1 km

N

4 TRAFFORD IN THE DARK AGES

The Romans left by AD410,[22] the trappings of civilisation disappeared and the area became partly reforested, probably occupied by the Romanised British (or Celts)[23] who inhabited a wide district round Eccles,[24] the parish of which included north Trafford. There are only two Celtic names left in Trafford, the Bollin and Mersey,[25] suggesting Trafford was partly deserted. The chiefdoms of the British land of Trafford were subsequently infiltrated by Anglo-Saxon farmers from Mercia[26] settling among the Britons. After AD678 the Mersey valley became the frontier between the Northumbrians and Mercians.[27] The Anglo-Saxon lands were divided for administration into Hundreds. The land north of the Mersey was part of Salford Hundred,[28] that to the south, part of Bucklow Hundred. The date of a long ditch, the Carr or Nico Ditch[29] built across north Trafford is unknown; it may have been a boundary between two British tribes, or between British and Anglo-Saxons, or Northumbrians and Mercians. From the mid-ninth century there were raids by Scandinavian Norsemen and in AD902 they attempted to invade the Mersey valley from the west. The Saxons, to protect themselves, then fortified a number of places including Manchester, and 'Weardbyrig' (915), possibly Warburton.[30] However, north Trafford was successfully settled by Scandinavians from the opposite direction, Danish invaders from east of the Pennines[31] who possibly founded Urmston, Flixton and Davyhulme perhaps on land cleared in Romano-British times.

Place-name meanings, **Fig. 4**, suggest the first Anglo-Saxon foundations in the mid-seventh century,[32] included Altrincham ('homestead or village of an 'inga' or tribal group of Aldhere', Aldhere's-inga-ham) and Dunham, Bowdon and Hale which referred to the hilly nature of the Altrincham ridge. Higham thinks Dunham and Bowdon were linked in a Saxon estate by having in their names the element 'dun' meaning 'hill'.[33] Kenyon thinks the 'ham' element refers to a place in an estate,[34] possibly formerly Romano-British. It is likely the incomers settled among the Britons by offering service to the local British chief. The Saxons lived in nucleated hamlets or villages, though a number of early non-nucleated places, such as Lostock, and Sale suggests some Celtic types of settlement were adopted by the Saxons. The second foundations may have been Warburton, Partington and Carrington, farmsteads ('tuns') with founders' names. Stretford and Old Trafford (both meaning 'street at the ford'), Dumplington, Lostock ('pigsty-place') and Whittleswick[35] may also be of this phase. A third stage of settlement was into clearings in woodland, for example, at Timperley ('timber-glade'),[36] Ashton, Sale and Alretunstall (now missing); the last three contain 'ash', 'willow' and, 'alder' suggesting the land needed clearance for agriculture to take place. The fourth foundations occurred when Danes occupied north Trafford at the beginning of the tenth century. Davyhulme refers to the lonely position of that place. The resulting pattern[37] was a polka-dot scatter of settlements in two zones: from Hale to Dunham and across north Trafford; and a linear pattern along the Mersey valley from Sale to Warburton.[38]

Not all modern places are on their original sites. Dore suggested that the early centre of Hale was originally in the Queens Road area;[39] not on Ashley Road; in this atlas its suggested location was Hale Barns on the main ancient ridgeway. Pryor thought Timperley was originally on Wood Lane,[40] not round the present crossroads. Swain placed old Sale on Dane Road.[41]

The lack of pagan Saxon burials suggests the area was Celtic Christian in the early Dark Ages. The huge parish of Bowdon included at least thirteen townships (Warburton was later separated from it). It had a church before Domesday, a dedication to St Mary and a churchyard of a subcircular shape, an early type suggesting it was an ancient focus for a Celtic area before Saxon times. Its imposing site is at 66 metres above sea-level.

Higham suggests much of south Trafford lay in one Saxon estate, coincident with most of Bowdon parish. Nine manors are mentioned in the Domesday Book (AD1086) as being owned in 1066 by Alfward, a Saxon thane, with his centre at Dunham. It had a resource centre (a mainly food producing place)[42] probably at Hale, possibly a defended Saxon hall at Dunham and a church at Bowdon. About 980 the Mercians parcelled twelve hundreds south of the Mersey into a shire, Legeceaster (Cheshire),[43] and the Mersey ('boundary river') became a shire boundary which would last almost a thousand years.

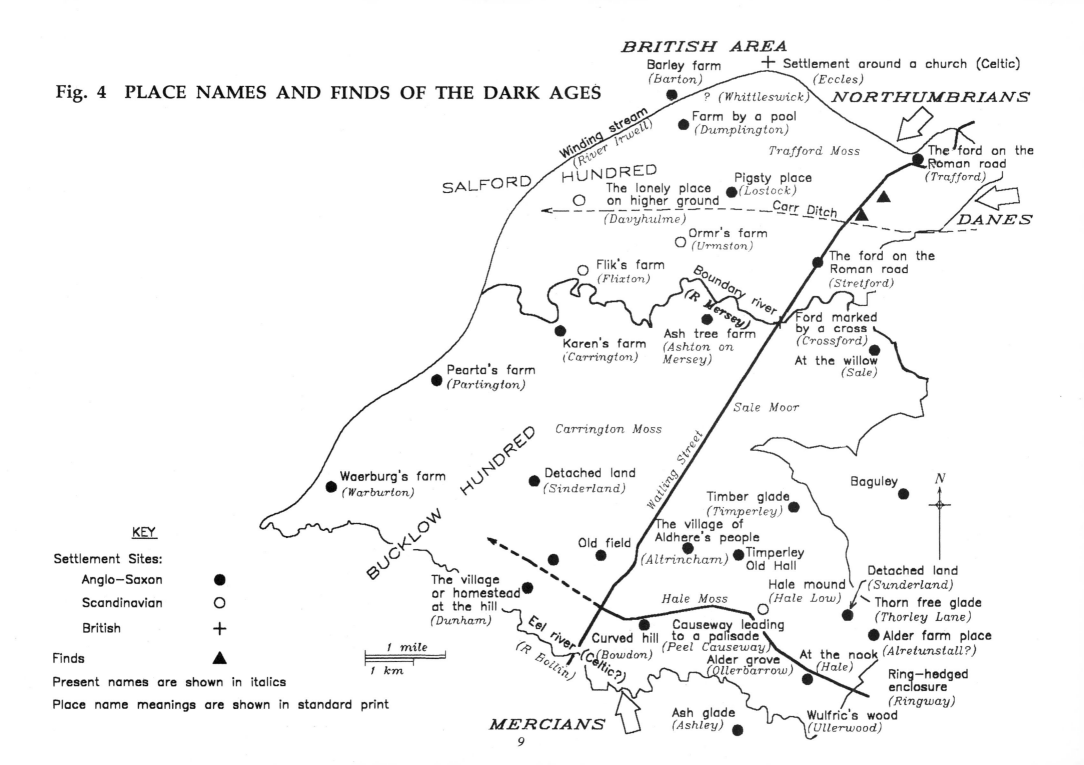

Fig. 4 PLACE NAMES AND FINDS OF THE DARK AGES

9

5 NORMAN TIMES

William the Norman conquered Cestrescire (Legeceaster – Cheshire) in AD1069-70 by a ruthless campaign called the 'harrying of the north' designed to punish the rebellious Earl Edwin of Mercia.[44] It succeeded in destroying or 'wasting' many manors in north Cheshire. None of the Saxon thanes was left in control of a manor and there was probably general slaughter. The 1086 tax inventory called the Domesday Book gives details of only a few places in Trafford.[45] There is no information for Altrincham, Ashton-on-Mersey, Carrington, Partington and Sale in south Trafford. Salford Hundred had over thirty manors including those of north Trafford but no details were given. Either the places had been obliterated or their details were included within those of larger manors. The places mentioned formed a linear pattern: Hale, Warburton, Dunham, Bowdon, Sunderland and Alretunstall (now lost). All except Warburton were lands given by the Norman Earl of Chester, Hugh Lupus,[46] to one of his barons, Hamon de Massey, who received almost the whole of south Trafford.[47]

In **Fig. 5a** in each place, except Warburton, the Saxon lord in 1066 had been a thane called Alfward and after 1070 its lord was the Norman baron Hamon de Massey based at Dunham. It is likely Hamon's estate also included Partington, Carrington, Sinderland, Ashton, Sale, Altrincham and Stretford (held by the Masseys till mid-twelfth century) as sub-manors of Dunham; and Timperley, Sunderland and Alretunstall as sub-manors of Hale. Urmston, Flixton, Davyhulme, Whittleswick, Lostock, Dumplington and Bromyhurst were sub-manors of Barton, which itself was held of Manchester. Warburton consisted of two manors. One had belonged to Ernwy and the other to Raven in Saxon times, and after the invasion of 1070 the former was given to the Norman baron William FitzNigel and the latter to Osbern son of Tezzo. William FitzNigel had his caput at Halton Castle,[48] Hamon built a castle at Dunham,[49] to guard his lands from Warburton eastwards to Baguley. With another castle at 'Ullerwood'[50] (built probably by Hamon) and one built by a baron at Stockport,[51] the Bollin and Mersey lands from Halton to Stockport were watched from a string of Norman castles. A castle at Manchester controlled the Irwell valley and north Trafford.

Fig. 5b shows the population of the manors of south Trafford was only seventeen; if each person recorded represented a family of five people this was less than a hundred people. Two Frenchmen were recorded and a 'rider', minor knights or retainers, perhaps given land for army service or brought in to populate abandoned manors. The Saxon inhabitants seem to have been virtually wiped out by the savagery of the invasion. The values of the manors, apart from Bowdon and Alretunstall, showed a positive figure for AD1066, 'in the time of King Edward (the Confessor)'. Each manor was 'waste' between 1066 and 1086 during which time the invasion took place. By 1086, each manor, apart from Alretunstall, Sunderland and possibly one of the Warburton manors had made some recovery. Bowdon was waste in 1066 when Alfward was alive. Had there been a revolt against him?

Fig. 5c shows arable land was reckoned in hides of 120 acres,[52] vills being assessed as parts or multiples of these.[53] Dunham and Hale had woodland, Hale a league (three miles). Hale was the 'resource centre' of the barony with a hawk's eyrie, an enclosure and meadow. Bowdon had a mill. The people of the manors could gather the products of the woods and mosslands: peat, wood, thatch and fowl.[54]

Dunham was the chief place where Hamon's motte-and-bailey castle (the site of which possibly lies adjacent to the present hall) may have been thrown up near a Saxon hall belonging to Alfward. Hamon also possessed a house in the city of Chester associated with membership of Hugh Lupus' council. The fact that Hamon was not given a (salt) house in the 'wiches' like other barons, suggests he was able to use local brine springs in the Bollin valley. South Trafford, a Saxon estate coincident with the ancient parish of Bowdon had been transferred intact to Norman ownership with its fortified administrative centre, Dunham. The Dunham estate was mirrored on the north side of the Mersey by a similar estate based on Salford which had a resource centre with enclosures, a hawk's eyrie and a league of woodland – interestingly, a similar list to that of Hale. Though not mentioned in Domesday Book, it is believed (Old) Trafford was in existence, a sub-manor of Manchester held by the de Trafford family from before Norman times. The family was to give its name over nine hundred years later to Trafford Metropolitan Borough.

Fig. 5 FEATURES FROM DOMESDAY BOOK

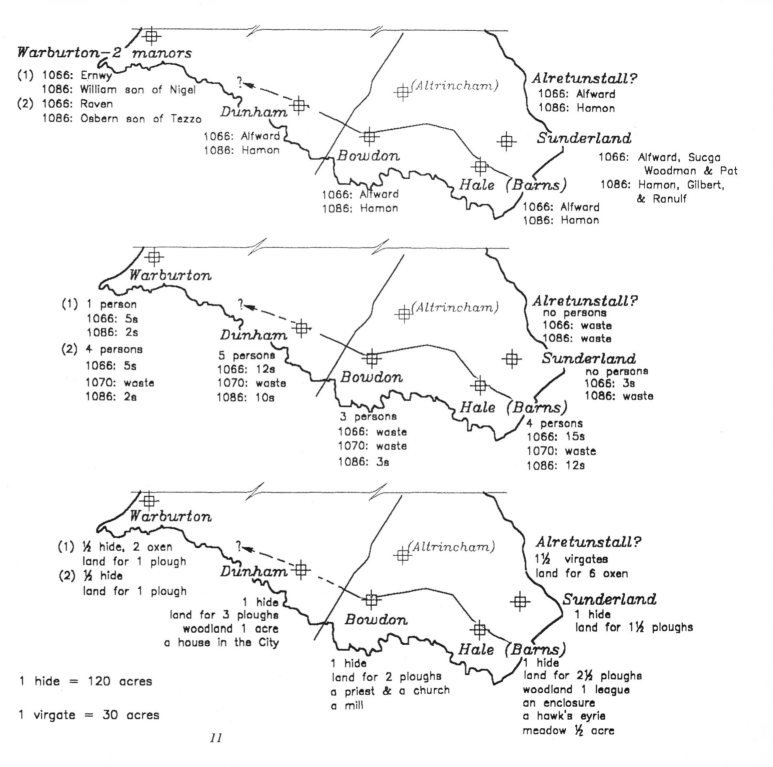

a Manors and Owners in 1066 and 1086

Warburton—2 manors
(1) 1066: Ernwy
    1086: William son of Nigel
(2) 1066: Raven
    1086: Osbern son of Tezzo

Dunham
1066: Alfward
1086: Hamon

(Altrincham)

Bowdon
1066: Alfward
1086: Hamon

Hale (Barns)
1066: Alfward
1086: Hamon

Alretunstall?
1066: Alfward
1086: Hamon

Sunderland
1066: Alfward, Sucga, Woodman & Pat
1086: Hamon, Gilbert, & Ranulf

b Population and Value of Manors

Warburton
(1) 1 person
    1066: 5s
    1086: 2s
(2) 4 persons
    1066: 5s
    1070: waste
    1086: 2s

Dunham
5 persons
1066: 12s
1070: waste
1086: 10s

(Altrincham)

Bowdon
3 persons
1066: waste
1070: waste
1086: 3s

Hale (Barns)
4 persons
1066: 15s
1070: waste
1086: 12s

Alretunstall?
no persons
1066: waste
1086: waste

Sunderland
no persons
1066: 3s
1086: waste

c Land and Other Features

Warburton
(1) ½ hide, 2 oxen
    land for 1 plough
(2) ½ hide
    land for 1 plough

Dunham
1 hide
land for 3 ploughs
woodland 1 acre
a house in the City

(Altrincham)

Bowdon
1 hide
land for 2 ploughs
a priest & a church
a mill

Hale (Barns)
1 hide
land for 2½ ploughs
woodland 1 league
an enclosure
a hawk's eyrie
meadow ½ acre

Alretunstall?
1½ virgates
land for 6 oxen

Sunderland
1 hide
land for 1½ ploughs

1 hide = 120 acres

1 virgate = 30 acres

6 FROM NORMAN TIMES TO 1500

During the first two centuries to AD1300 population, economic and military activity increased greatly with baronial wars and wars against the Scots and Welsh.[55] Powerful Anglo-Norman families played an early version of Monopoly to grasp, physically or by marriage dower, what lands they could from each other. Many places were assessed as military fiefs. Barton, extending over north Trafford, was held for two knights' fees, of which one Urmston lord held one eighth and a Flixton lord one sixth of a fee,[56] all under the Baron of Manchester. In the south, Dunham was the focus, where by an edict of AD1288[57] the fifth Hamon de Massey had to find five knights' fees for the Earl of Chester from his manors: for example, Sale and Ashton had to provide fees of one and a tenth knights and the lords of Carrington were to provide two parts of a knight's fee in order to hold Carrington, half of Ashton and a third of Partington. The knights so furnished were not only used against the Welsh but also in defending the castles along the Bollin (at Dunham, Watch Hill, and Ullerwood), for example, in a revolt involving the Masseys against Henry II in 1173.[58] In the following two centuries to 1500, particularly after the Black Death of 1348-49, there was a decline in both military activity and population.[59]

From before Domesday, Cheshire (south Trafford) was governed from Chester Castle, but administration of Lancashire (north Trafford) from Lancaster Castle was not mentioned until AD1182.[60] In fact the land 'between the Ribble and Mersey' was still in the Earl of Chester's hands in 1232.[61] Hamon de Massey IV had lands in north Trafford. In 1250 he gave Stretford as dowry to his daughter Margery[62] and they passed to the de Trafford family. Lancashire began its palatine independence in 1182 while Cheshire continued from 980.

Fig. 6 shows the settlement pattern continued as small nucleated vills (villages or hamlets).[63] Halls were found in the larger vills; other halls outside the vills may have been estates belonging to knightly retainers. Each lord would have some type of palisaded[64] or moated hall. Richard 'del Bonk' lived in Bank Hall, Hale in 1348. The wealthier lords created palisaded deer parks for hunting at Dunham,[65] Warburton,[66] Sunderland[67] and near Old Trafford Hall.[68] At the beginning of the period the common people lived in a system of tight feudal control under local military lords, themselves owing suit and service to major magnates. Each vill lay in a township, an area which contained a variety of land-use: such as arable, pasture, meadow, woodland, moss, moor and water. The land was worked partly by freemen and partly by communal organisation of villeins, who paid dues to the lord, or worked his lands. The term 'field' usually indicates former communal agriculture, or physical evidence of former stripfields, as in areas shown on the map. There is evidence of usually one main openfield, the 'townfield',[69] divided into strips probably allocated each year to different tenants and cultivated communally by a shared plough. There was communal woodland where those with rights could get wood for enclosures, house building, fires and carts. There was peat from the mosses and moors (turbary) and common meadows divided into strips.

The notion of self-contained vills does not seem to be the whole picture because the lords called on individual places for different specialisations. For example, some vills such as Bowdon, Flixton and Warburton had churches; several had mills. Dunham was an administrative centre and also had a coney warren. Dumplington also had a warren. Baguley (then in Bucklow)[70] had the task of fetching salt from the 'wiches'. Altrincham was noted for pigs.[71] the family at Bowdon Hall became involved in estate administration.[72] Urmston had to find a fourth part of a sergeant or judge.[73] Seen as a whole pattern, an estate was an organised entity with each place having a function. There were outlying estates farmed by freemen, or military retainers in new halls, and demesnes farmed by bailiffs for the lord. There was hunting with hawks in Hale[74] and in Salford Hundred (which included north Trafford).[75] Some places had greens and open areas, such as Sunderland, and were concerned with demesne animal stocks. The lands of south Trafford continued to be overseen for a short time by the castles strung out along the Bollin valley; the lands in the north were watched over by a defended place, perhaps a fortified manor house, at Manchester. A distinctive pattern was made by the many mills strung out along the Mersey and Bollin like beads on a string.

It seems the corn-based manorial existence went on alongside another economy concerned with the provision of meat and other products probably from huge grazing grounds, some of which were

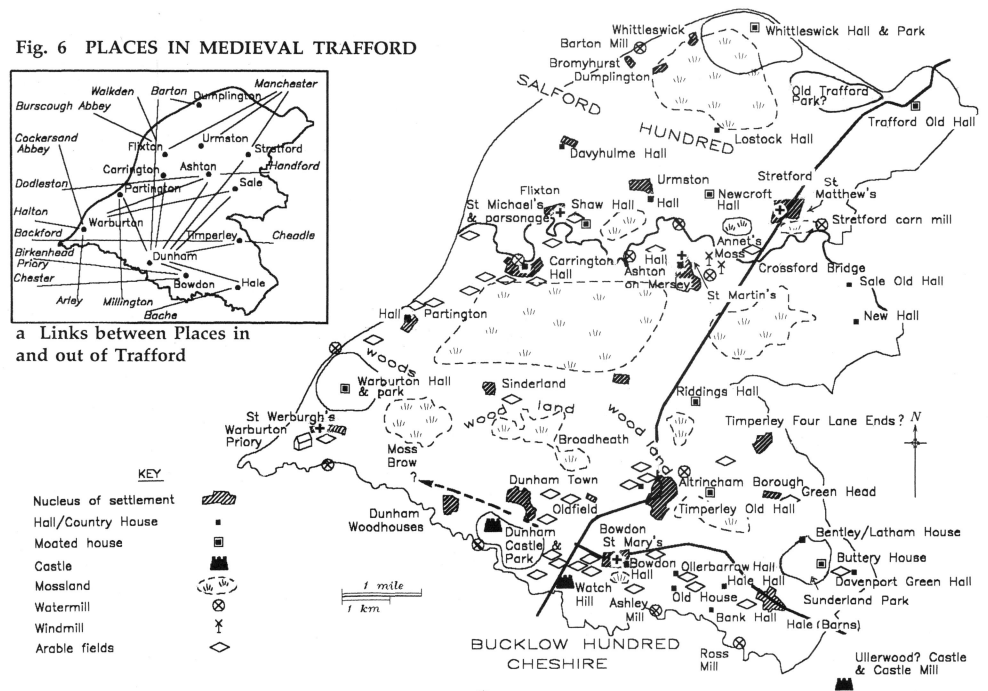

Fig. 6 PLACES IN MEDIEVAL TRAFFORD

a Links between Places in and out of Trafford

Inset map labels: Walkden, Barton, Manchester, Dumplington, Burscough Abbey, Cockersand Abbey, Flixton, Urmston, Stretford, Dodleston, Carrington, Ashton, Handford, Halton, Partington, Sale, Backford, Warburton, Birkenhead Priory, Chester, Dunham, Timperley, Cheadle, Arley, Millington, Bowdon, Hale, Bache

KEY

	Nucleus of settlement
▪	Hall/Country House
▣	Moated house
♜	Castle
	Mossland
⊗	Watermill
✗	Windmill
◇	Arable fields

Map labels: Whittleswick, Whittleswick Hall & Park, Barton Mill, Bromyhurst, Dumplington, SALFORD HUNDRED, Old Trafford Park?, Trafford Old Hall, Lostock Hall, Davyhulme Hall, Urmston Hall, Flixton, St Michael's & parsonage, Shaw Hall, Newcroft Hall, Stretford, St Matthew's, Stretford corn mill, Annet's Moss, Carrington Hall, Hall, Ashton on Mersey, Crossford Bridge, St Martin's, Sale Old Hall, New Hall, Hall Partington, woods, woodland, Warburton Hall & park, Sinderland, Riddings Hall, St Werburgh's Warburton Priory, Broadheath, Timperley Four Lane Ends?, N, Moss Brow?, Dunham Town, Altrincham Borough, Green Head, Oldfield, Timperley Old Hall, Dunham Woodhouses, Bentley/Latham House, Bowdon St Mary's, Buttery House, Dunham Castle & Park, Bowdon Hall, Ollerbarraw Hall, Davenport Green Hall, Watch Hill, Hale Hall, Sunderland Park, Ashley Mill, Old House, Bank Hall, Hale (Barns), BUCKLOW HUNDRED CHESHIRE, Ross Mill, Ullerwood? Castle & Castle Mill

1 mile / 1 km

demesne pastures, interlinked with a number of 'greens' described later in the atlas. Changes took place: Sinderland, a large heath, including peat bog and woodland was enclosed after 1290 probably for grazing, Riddings ('clearings' from mossland) appeared in Timperley.[76] Gradually more land was leased or sold to individual farmers.

The Saxon system of local administration continued. The manor was not only a feudal land holding, its lord had jurisdiction over its inhabitants. The lord of a place such as Dunham held a halmote, later a court leet,[77] once or twice a year to organise officials, keep a census of people and try small offences, the worst offences being tried at the Hundred Court and County Assize. A court baron met every three weeks to try minor offences, for example, at Stretford.[78] Later the de Massey manors paid suit and service to the Court Leet and View of Frankpledge of Dunham (the barony court) and to Bucklow Hundred Court; those north of the Mersey to the court leet at Manchester (the barony court) and Salford Hundred Court.[79]

In the early part of this period there was a spate of ecclesiastical building. The edifices were erected by wealthy lords (in some cases to expiate their sins on earth). Monasteries were usually built in the lords' out-of-the-way manors. For their upkeep, the institutions were frequently given monies received by churches and manors located near the home base of the lord. So military and economic feudalism ran parallel to ecclesiastical organisation. There were major churches at Eccles, Manchester and Bowdon. The domains of the first two churches were divided from that of Bowdon by the Mersey valley. Manchester parish included Trafford and Stretford. Flixton parish, which included Urmston, was carved out of that of Eccles[80] and St Michael's church, Flixton, was given to Burscough priory in AD1189[81] or 1190. St Martin's, Ashton-on-Mersey, became a parish, created out of Bowdon, in 1304[82] to serve also Carrington and Sale. St Matthew's, a chapel-at-ease of Manchester, was built at Stretford in 1413.[83] Two churches in the south had links outside the Trafford area. Bowdon church owned land in one moiety of the manor of Bowdon and in 1278 its advowson, and half an acre in Dunham Massey were given to Birkenhead Priory, a Massey foundation of 1150.[84] Warburton had two manors, in one of which there was a chapel dedicated to St Wearburgh, a Mercian princess, perhaps through a similarity of name.[85] In 1190 a priory was built there for Norbertine Premonstratensian canons who later moved to

Cockersand and the land was sold back to Geoffrey de Dutton of Warburton in 1271.[86]

Mention must be made of the foundation of the borough of Altrincham in 1290 which introduced urban living to Trafford. Elsewhere there was only a handful of places we would today regard as villages: Stretford, Bowdon, Dunham Town, Flixton and Ashton. The rest of the settlements were scattered halls and hamlets.

In the inset map the complicated pattern of internal and external connections between places can be seen, due to landlords' possessions, obligations and gifts. The contrast was between places north of, and places south of the Mersey. Places north of the Mersey had connections outwards as tenants of the Grelleys, overlords of Manchester, or the Booths of Barton and the Radcliffes;[87] there was also a more distant religious link between Flixton and Burscough. Most manors in south Trafford focused radially inwards on Dunham. In the mid-fourteenth century the Masseys of Dunham were replaced by external lords, the Fittons of Wilmslow and the Duke of Lancaster. From the mid-fifteenth century the Booth family owned Dunham, though it is doubtful if they took up residence before 1500.[88]

In the south, there were also wide external contacts. Ashton was linked to the Boydells of Dodleston, the Breretons of Handford and the Venables of Kinderton; Timperley was linked to the Ardernes of Backford and Buckleys of Cheadle; Hale was linked to the Venables, and Stanleys of Lathom and Chauntrells of Bache;[89] Sale and Warburton were linked to Halton through the Lestranges and to Arley through the de Duttons (Warburtons). There were links between Bowdon and Birkenhead, between Warburton, Lymm church, and (through the priory of St John of Jerusalem at Warburton) with Cockersand and Chester Abbey. The former self-contained estate relationships of Saxon times had changed.

North and south Trafford to some extent mirrored each other. They lay in different counties, in different hundreds and each became dominated by an estate headed by a powerful family. Each estate was centred on a hall, possessed a deer park and was supported by manors contributing specialisms which ranged from administration down to rabbit warrens. The different feature between north and south was the presence in the south of the borough of Altrincham.

7 TRAFFORD'S FIRST BOROUGH

A new way of life was introduced to Trafford in AD1290 – urban life. By royal and borough charters,[90] the town of Altrincham appeared on the scene, **Fig. 7**, showing a rectangular pattern of a planned grid-iron of streets next to a new-fangled permanent market. Other markets already existed at Manchester[91] and Stockport.[92] The new town seems to have been added to an existing village in Dunham township and completely occupied its lands. It lay squeezed between the old village fields on high ground and Hale Moss. Altrincham's foundation suggests the local manorial economy was insufficient to provide the needs of the military Dunham caput. It can be seen as a speculation not only to secure money for Hamon de Massey V who founded it[93] but to supplement the existing resource centre of Hale. Free burgesses (probably 120), mainly traders, were invited into the borough and given a burgage plot in the town. These form a striped pattern behind the houses. Instead of working the lord's land, the burgesses paid rent for a 1 acre strip in the town common field of the former village,[94] these are shown by the broad bands in the top left of the map. These they could dispose of at will (within constraints). There were meadows for reaping hay to the east along Timperley Brook. Because of a shortage of land the burgesses were given common of pasture for cattle and pigs and rights to turbary in Dunham and Timperley as well as on Hale Moss. The duty to attend the lord's halmote at Dunham was replaced by a traders' court in the market place, a portmote, which in the fourteenth century became a court leet; there was also a court of 'pie powder' to deal with offences committed at the fair.

The Black Death disaster of 1348-49 halved the population; in Altrincham at this date there were only forty-five burgesses cultivating 127 burgages.[95] Urbanism subsequently declined here as in other parts of England.[96] The numbers of tenants-at-will in Altrincham in 1500 had halved in a century to eight. It is unlikely other towns were developing in Trafford. The tendency was to revert in some ways to rural conditions.

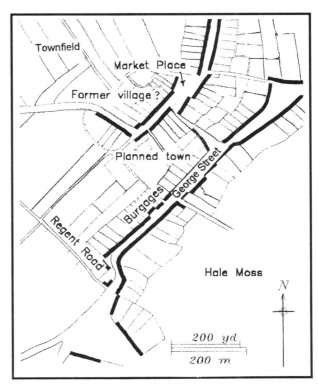

Fig. 7 IMAGINATIVE RECONSTRUCTION OF MEDIEVAL ALTRINCHAM

8 TRAFFORD IN THE EARLY SEVENTEENTH CENTURY

This small map, **Fig. 8**, is part of a composite of Speed's maps of Lancashire and Cheshire reproduced by Greater Manchester Council in 1975 before that body was abolished. The map is artistically attractive but not as informative as could be wished. In terms of physical geography there is no indication of height but the main streams are shown, the Irwell and Mersey together with the Sinderland, Timperley and Fairywell brooks. Though Chat Moss is shown on the Lancashire side of the Irwell, not one moss is shown in the Trafford area. Distances are subjective but, overall, give a reasonable idea of the relative position of places.

The map shows which places were considered to be important in James I's reign. There were three country houses with parks. Old ('Holme') Trafford is shown adjacent to a treeless park. This park is not the Trafford Park of later times but an earlier one which will be identified further on in this atlas. Warburton and Dunham parks are shown with trees in them. Sunderland park is not indicated therefore it must have been turned into farmland by this date. The symbol for Dunham Hall or Town is in the wrong place, perhaps for reasons of artistic licence, whereas the positions of the other two halls are shown relatively correctly. Altrincham's name is printed larger than that of Stretford, Ashton and Flixton because it was the largest place, but the drawn symbols for the last three places look more important than the symbol for Altrincham because they each had a church while Altrincham did not. The symbol for Flixton looks larger than that for Urmston and this reflects their relative importance at this date. There is no sign of Hale which is surprising when it has been assumed to have been very important and large in early times. In contrast 'Whickleswik', assumed to have been a small hamlet, is shown. 'Redings' (Riddings Hall) is evident but there is no sign of Timperley Old Hall or village.

Fig. 8 SPEED'S MAP OF 1610

9 EARLY LAW AND ADMINISTRATION

After medieval times, local law and administration continued to be carried out by the manor courts, variously called the court leet, view of frankpledge, or halmote (for example, at Urmston and Stretford). The Dunham court varied its name. In the fourteenth century it was a halmote, subsequently titled court leet, and occasionally, view of frankpledge or other title; the title court leet was commonly used from the eighteenth century. Altrincham in the barony of Dunham was given a portmote (traders' court) in 1290 but this later became a court leet. These courts met twice yearly interspersed with three-weekly 'court barons'. Altrincham had a court of pie powder which regulated the fair.

Trafford was divided for legal attendance by the Mersey. The main courts for northern Trafford (in Lancashire) were held at the hundred centre, Salford and at Manchester.[97] In south Trafford, those for the Dunham estates of the Booths were held at Altrincham courthouse. One manor of Warburton held court at Halton and Arley, the other manor had a court leet held by authority of the hospital of St John of Jerusalem (formerly at Warburton). At this time courts were run by magistrates or special officers rather than estate officers.[98] The view of frankpledge (court leet), Fig. 9, included a roll call of all major land holders. Such notables did not do jury duty nor take on administrative service (swine looker, constable, etc.) which was left to the locals. The map shows a radial pattern of links between south Trafford and north Cheshire.

Increase of population at the same time as enclosure of the commons led to several intertwined events reflected in cases brought to the courts. Enclosure led to less land being available to the commoners. The courts tightened regulations to preserve the rights of the remaining commoners to the reduced amount of arable, pasture, wood and waste. Court rolls of the Tudor and Jacobean periods are crammed with complaints against individuals for not doing necessary ditching or for grazing too many animals on the shrinking commons. Some people were left without land which led to increased vagrancy and violence and workhouses were built, for example, at Altrincham in 1756.[99] Attacks on the person were mentioned frequently. Control by unpaid officers was becoming difficult, the ancient local government-judicial system was beginning to break down.

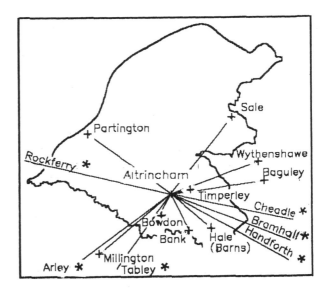

knights   *

squires   +

Fig. 9 HOME BASES OF THOSE CALLED TO THE VIEW OF FRANKPLEDGE OF SIR GEORGE BOOTH OF DUNHAM 1610

Following the decline of population until about 1500, numbers subsequently increased through the Tudor period. This led to cheap labour and the reimposition of manorial service on many people who could not hold their land.[100] The number of squires declined and acquisition of some of their properties led to the creation of two dominant gentlemen's estates, Dunham Hall and Trafford Hall. Freeholding, leaseholding and copyholding were the normal types of tenancy. One body of freeholders was in the chartered borough of Altrincham, other freeholders were found in the small estates and some were well-to-do independents and farmers called charterers. Leaseholders were, in the main, yeomen, who possessed property for up to three lives.[101] Copyholders were tenants-at-will, with obligations to the lord, including a heriot (a fine, usually money or the 'best beast') payable on death.

The principle of commonfield farming for the villagers was that of the dole system involving the annual allocation of scattered unfenced strips (loonts or butts) which had been worked in common from the medieval period, in patches of land separated by mearestones. These lands usually lay in one great town field (and in some places smaller fields) close to the village. Though no doubt rotated in early times (except at Altrincham), as time passed tenancy became fixed[102] though there is evidence of the openfield system still operating in Dumplington and Stretford in the seventeenth century.[103] By the eighteenth century all loonts had been allocated with agreement of the landlords and enclosed. Yeomanry, estate working, and small-scale farming increased and communal farming waned. By the time of the tithe maps in the early nineteenth century several places showed only vestiges of the shapes of former openfield. New techniques were spreading, for example, productivity was raised by the use of marl, a limy clay found among the boulder clay. A study of Dunham by Littler[104] shows that the early eighteenth century experienced a revival of manorialism leading to increased pressure on tenants to perform duties or 'boons' or pay monies in lieu, but by the end of the eighteenth century these had

been discontinued.

A wide range of social classes developed reflected in their type of abode: the nobility – Dunham Hall; the squires and some freehold charterers – other halls and large farms; yeomen – farms; charterers – large houses and farms; copyholders and renters in the villages and hamlets – small farms; town dwellers in Altrincham and, by the end of the eighteenth century, Stretford: professional men (some to deal with the innumerable land transfers taking place) – large town houses; tradesmen – shops and workshops; menials and beggars – hovels.

By 1800 there were churches at Bowdon, Ashton-on-Mersey, Warburton and Flixton and chapels-of-ease at Stretford (Manchester parish), Altrincham (Bowdon parish) and Carrington (Bowdon parish). Dissenting chapels could be found at Altrincham, Ringway to 1723 and at Hale from 1723,[105] Partington and Stretford. The presence of a church or chapel does not seem to have led to significant village growth, but might have reflected growth.

This period saw the felling of most of the remaining woodland and major encroachments into and enclosure of heath and peat moss for arable and pasture. The drainage of parts of Trafford Moss was sanctioned by Act of Parliament in 1793[106] and Sale Moor in 1806.[107] At Dunham, the increasing manorial control[108] led to a surplus of wealth and enabled a rebuilding of the hall between 1720 and 1740. The de Traffords' hall at Old Trafford was abandoned by that family who moved two miles away to a new hall in 1720, shown in **Fig. 10** as Trafford Hall[109] formerly Whittleswick Hall, which the family had owned since the previous century.

Fig. 10 is a composite map made from two eighteenth century maps.[110] It shows the meandering Irwell and Mersey which had in fact been improved for navigation and trade in the seventeenth century by being partly canalised as the Mersey and Irwell Navigation from 1734. The new Bridgewater Canal of 1761-5 is also shown. Two major estates of the Earls of Stamford and Warrington, and the de Traffords mirrored each other at the opposite ends of Trafford,

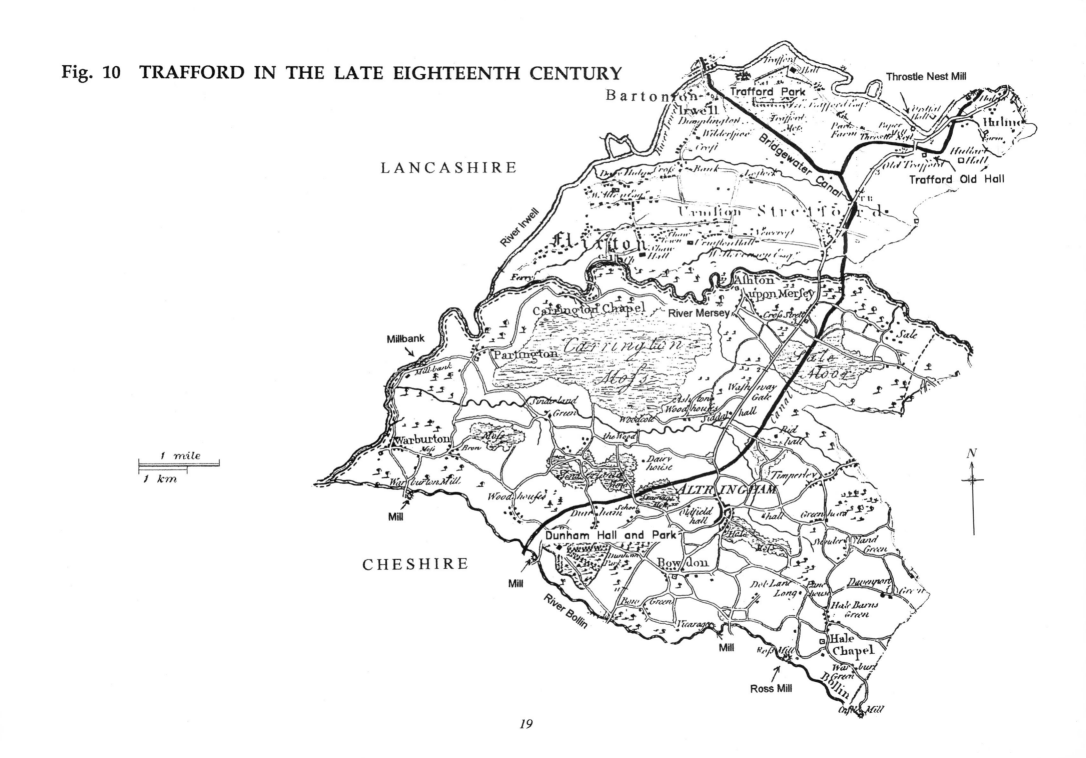

Fig. 10 TRAFFORD IN THE LATE EIGHTEENTH CENTURY

LANCASHIRE

CHESHIRE

Throstle Nest Mill

Trafford Park

Trafford Old Hall

Millbank

Carrington Chapel

River Mersey

Mill

Dunham Hall and Park

Mill

River Bollin

Ross Mill

Hale Chapel

1 mile

1 km

N

each with a river at one side and the Bridgewater Canal on the other. A large percentage of the area was still covered in mossland. Altrincham and Stretford were clearly urban. In addition to the original five villages (Ashton, Bowdon, Dunham, Flixton and Stretford) the following had grown into villages: Carrington, Dunham Woodhouses, Hale (Hale Barns or East Hale), Partington, Timperley, Urmston and Warburton. Villages and hamlets were either compact clusters of houses or linear street settlements. Those in the north – for example, Flixton, Davyhulme, Urmston, Shaw Town and Crofts Bank were street settlements, ribbon developments along pre-existing roads. In the south, the only compact clustered settlements were Warburton, Partington and Bowdon. The rest were street settlements: Carrington, Dunham Town, Dunham Woodhouses, Moss Brow, Green Head and Four Lane Ends (Timperley), Hale (Barns) and Ashton-on-Mersey. There were smaller hamlets both in the north and the south – Old Trafford, Dumplington, Whittleswick, Bromyhurst and in the south Sinderland Green, Ashton Woodhouses, Cross Street, and (old) Sale. Some places were probably newly developed such as Four Lane Ends (Timperley), Wilderspool, Crofts Bank, Ashton Woodhouses, Dunham Woodhouses, Moss Brow and Cross Street. The distance to Manchester might have had an influence on shape and size: the northern places being nearer to the metropolis developed textile outwork industries (for example, wool and fustian weaving) leading to the building of cottages along northern roads. The southern villages were more isolated from Manchester and remained smaller and more compact in shape. A pattern emerged of halls, villages and hamlets surrounded by dispersed or clustered farms. Many farms were built round the edges of Sale and Urmston moors and Carrington, Sinderland, Trafford and Warburton mosses. There were new large farms such as Siddall Hall. The several 'greens' of Trafford which had probably been earlier used in a pastoral economy were by now incorporated into local farms. Medieval Sunderland Park was now called Sunderland, or Davenport, Green and apportioned for farming.

Trafford was not by-passed by the industrial and communications revolution. There were eighteenth century paper mills at Throstle Nest (Old Trafford),[111] and Partington Millbank (where there was the first steam engine in the area by 1796),[112] replaced, on the same site by a slitting and rolling mill, a corn mill and again a paper mill before 1800. Most energy came from water, hand or horsepower. There were waterpowered corn mills on the Trafford side of the Irwell opposite Barton, on the Bollin at Dunham, Bowdon, Hale and Warburton and on the Mersey at Carrington and Ashton (not shown); but the former Mersey mills at Stretford, Urmston and Flixton had disappeared.[113] Altrincham mill has been mentioned. Ashton, Timperley and Carrington also had windmills for corn grinding (not shown on the map).[114] Most villages in this period had tradesmen and craftsmen such as smiths, spinners and weavers of hemp and wool (for example, the Dunham area and Urmston).[115] Altrincham was noted for domestic spinning and weaving.[116] There were tanyards in Partington, Flixton, Hale and Altrincham (indicated by fieldnames). Salt brine production was important in the west Bollin valley at Dunham and Dunham Woodhouses.[117] There was quarrying of the Keuper sandstones at Timperley for stone for the bases of wood-framed houses and claypits in the boulder clay areas of south Trafford were stimulated by the need for bricks in the Great Rebuilding and the spread of farmsteads. A longstanding agricultural industry, dairying, was related to the adoption of ringfenced farms and boosted by the building of a buttermarket in Altrincham in 1684.

Watling Street was turnpiked in 1752 and the Bridgewater Canal was completed through Trafford in 1765.[118] The canal carried cargoes of stone, marl and lime (to improve the heaths and mosslands), wood, wool and cotton yarn and cloth, coal and nightsoil. Sale may qualify as being the only new canal town of Trafford; its centre moved from the Dane Road area to around the canal bridge (subsequent to the date of **Fig. 10** of 1777) and, with Stretford, it began to increase in size through trade from the canal wharves. Broadheath became a small port for Altrincham, with a warehouse and boatshed, from where small-scale commuting to Manchester by canal boat began.[119] The canal contributed wealth leading to another phase of urban rebuilding in the late eighteenth century.[120] The turnpike and canal of eastern Trafford encouraged the build-up of trade and populations along the corridor from Manchester to the south-west.

11 WARBURTON IN 1757

Warburton township was situated round St Werburgh's church on a bluff overlooking the Mersey between the Red Brook and the Bollin. In the north, west and south streams formed natural boundaries while to the east were Warburton Moss and carr land (heath) towards Dunham Massey. The redrafted Arley estates map[121] reproduced here shows the site of Warburton Hall and Park. Field patterns include loonts (strips) in the former Townfield and another, smaller openfield. The patchwork of new fields and zigzag tracks arose from piecemeal enclosure of the former moss which once extended to the surrounding road. The inhabitants of the daughter hamlet of Moss Brow may have begun the enclosure of the moss. There are large fields enclosed from the former deer park, strips in common meadow near the river and rectangular enclosures of carr heath in the east.

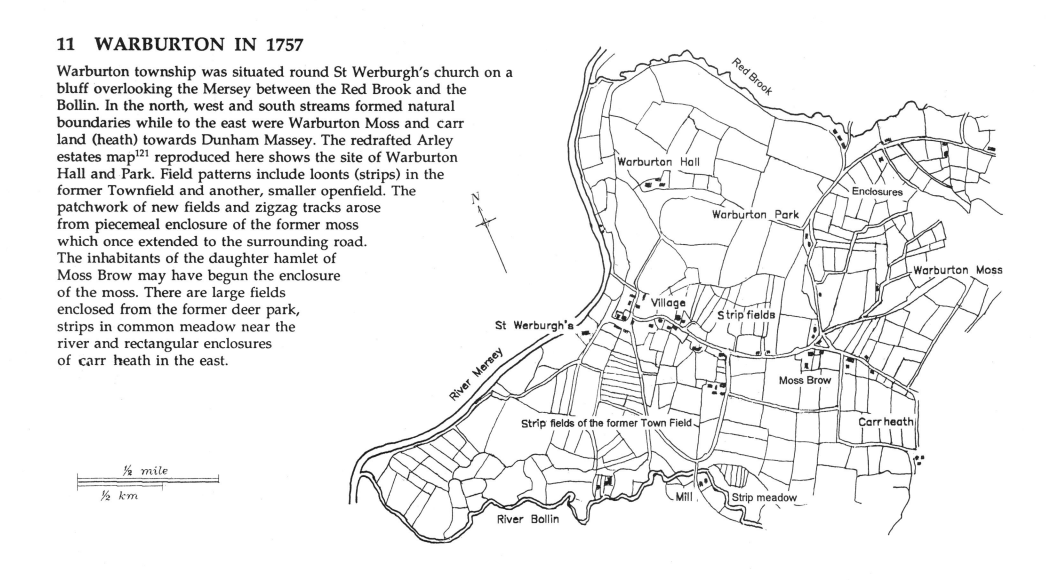

Fig. 11 FIELD PATTERNS IN WARBURTON

12   ALTRINCHAM TOWNSHIP AND TOWN IN 1799

The estate map, **Fig. 12**, shows the holdings in Altrincham of the Booths of Dunham (in the person of the Earl of Warrington) who owned over half the township and two-thirds of the town.[122] The lack of detail in some parts of the map represents properties not owned by the Earl. Altrincham township (the borough of 1290) included part of Oldfield hamlet, shown as the lands of Oldfield Hall (seventeenth century).

Altrincham grew slightly from 1000 people in 1750 to 1029 in 1772[123] and then dramatically to 1692 in 1801.[124] One factor which helped it to grow suddenly was the turnpiking of the stage routes through it into Cheshire, but the chief reason was the effect of the building of the Bridgewater Canal in 1765. On **Fig. 12** the small wharf-hamlet of Broadheath can be seen. Of no great size at this period, it was, nevertheless, vital in bringing cheap coal for one or two textile factories in Altrincham (not shown), bringing corn and increasing the supply of wool and cotton yarn for domestic processing. The canal also brought night-soil from Manchester for the new orchard-crop and vegetable growing industry and provided transport to market for the vegetables and orchard products when grown; and was an outlet for the sandstone of Timperley. The economy was stimulated and population grew.

The large irregular fields in the north can be seen to have been cut through by, and therefore pre-date, the canal.[125] The field patterns of the township reflect the input of labour into them. Intensively-farmed gardens, small fields and closes surrounded the town on both sides. On the edges of the township lay large fields, extensively-farmed arable and pasture, with some meadows along the eastern boundary, Timperley Brook. West of the town the medieval pattern of strips of the huge Town Field which stretched from Oldfield Hall grounds to the Downs had become fossilised, being early enclosed and allocated to individuals from 1290. Several had been partitioned into market gardens. Most of the farms were in the town. Dairy herds flourished and much trade was done through the buttermarket. Hale Moss was still extensive and unenclosed, used for grazing cattle and horses.

The town was noted for its courts for the Dunham estates and those of the borough held in the courthouse in the market place, seen in the enlarged map Fig. 12a of the town centre, when the town would be particularly busy. An increase of wealth together with the dilapidation of old half-timbered and mud-walled houses led to a 'Great Rebuilding' of farms and town buildings in brick mainly in the period 1680-1720.[126] The Booths instituted some rebuilding of the centre especially in High Street (Market Street) after this period, including refacing timbered properties with Georgian fronts in Old Market Place. Here, in the economic centre of the borough, were several inns used by stage coaches. St George's had been built in 1799, a chapel-of-ease for Bowdon. Note that it was separated from Church Street by market gardens (which later disappeared for road widening). The town was noted for combed worsted and home stuffs. On what is now Grosvenor Road there was an ancient water-powered corn mill on a leet from Hale Moss. The town map also shows the ancient burgages still clearly visible around the medieval grid pattern of streets.[127] These were 2 Cheshire perches in width by 5 in length (120 feet by 24). The Market Street to Regent Road length of the grid was devoid of houses and gaps elsewhere between some of the houses suggest there had once been more dwellings and that the town was spatially smaller in 1799 than in previous times. High class Upper Altrincham around Old Market Place and Market Street was geographically, and socially, higher than, and clearly separated from, low class Lower Altrincham along George Street and Goose Green.

Fig. 12 ALTRINCHAM TOWNSHIP IN 1799

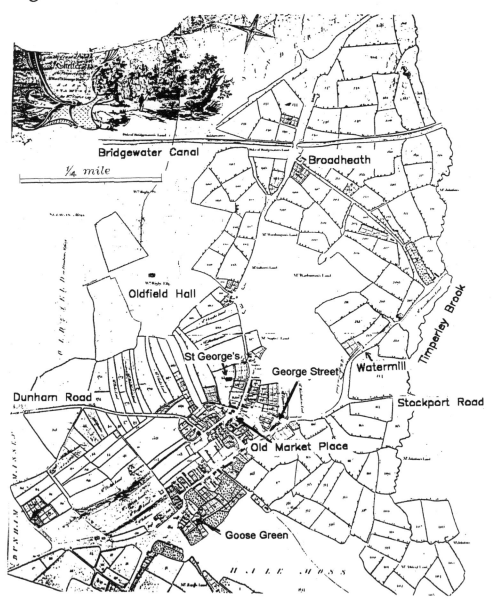

Bridgewater Canal

¼ mile

Broadheath

Oldfield Hall

Timperley Brook

St George's

George Street

Watermill

Dunham Road

Stockport Road

Old Market Place

Goose Green

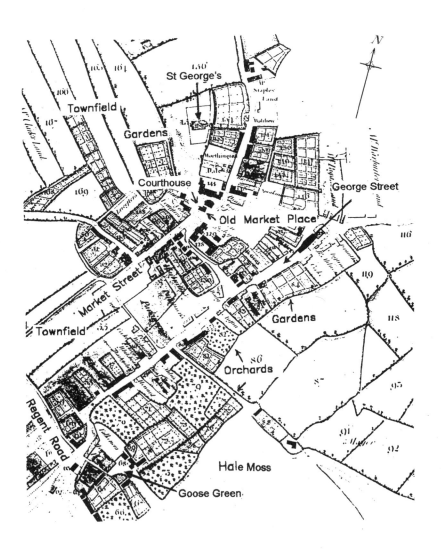

a Altrincham Town

13 DISCOVERING A LOST MEDIEVAL PARK

Part of a map from a survey in 1782 for John Trafford of his vast estate in north Trafford and across the Irwell is shown in **Fig. 13**. The estate was formerly based at Old Trafford Hall but the de Traffords had moved two miles west to a new hall in a spacious park in the manor of Whittleswick in 1720, possibly to get away from the bustle of the Chester road which passed in front of the old hall. This map shows Trafford Old Hall in the top right corner. Across the Chester road lay part of the estate divided by the line of the Bridgewater Canal on its way from Watersmeet, bottom right hand corner, to Manchester. A group of fields shaped like a distorted oval, with a farm, Park House, at its centre has been outlined in dots by the writer. Nearly all of this was tenanted by the occupants of Park House except that east of the canal they held only the two large fields Nearer and Farther Marl(e)d Rough. The suggestion is made here that at one time, well before the canal was cut, the whole oval was one huge parcel of open land and that this was the park of Trafford Old Hall. The name Park House suggests the farm was indeed in the former park. Formerly open land and a deer park, the park had been enclosed for farming by 1782.

It is fascinating to locate a former park but additionally its oval shape is similar to other large open spaces in northern England. Such an 'oval' can be linked with recent research and this may help to explain the presence and shape of the several former estate parks in Trafford. Human settlement rarely took place in a virgin environment, absolutely devoid of people. The Normans who came into Trafford are credited with the introduction of parks (as well as the manorial system and castles) but these had to be fitted into an existing Anglo-Saxon landscape. How was this done? Was there virgin woodland which had to be cleared? Or were existing villages cleared away as happened in medieval times at Tatton?[128] Research in more northern areas of Lancashire by Atkin[129] has revealed an ancient set of field patterns consisting of huge oval-shaped open lands connected by paths. The case is made out that the first phase of ancient settlement into wooded areas involved clearance of swathes of ground in sub-circular shapes, now shown by curved field boundaries, called by Atkin 'ovals', within which arable cultivation or pasturing could be carried out. These large open spaces were there when the Normans came and may be even pre-Saxon. Several features in Trafford resemble 'oval' field shapes similar to that in the map. Field names in them suggest they were part of such a system used for both arable and pasture, with the emphasis on pasture. The animals provided meat, dairy products and plough-beasts for the lord, as part of his demesne.

This animal culture, it is suggested, was part of an economy which centuries ago provided meat on the hoof from distant manors and for the south of England.[130] To move the animals, drovers' roads were essential. The writer suggests that Watling Street was such a drovers' road from Old Trafford. The existence of other 'ovals' will be considered later in this atlas.

Fig. 13   PART OF A MAP OF THE ESTATES OF JOHN TRAFFORD IN 1782

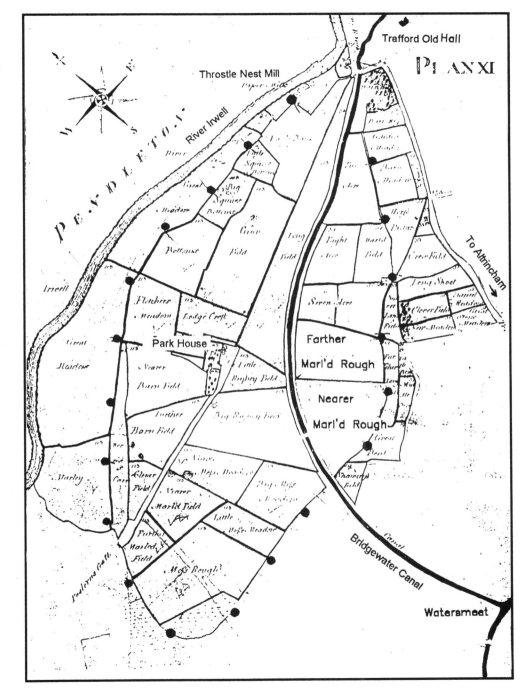

200 yd

200 m

14 TOWNSHIPS OF TRAFFORD UP TO 1800

Townships were tracts of land needed by settlements to support their inhabitants, originally by farming. They were areas, each of which contained a similar variety of soil quality and other characteristics but might vary in size. The size of the township reflected the quality of the resources and the size of the community. Townships in poor soil areas tended to be large to provide for a population which in richer areas could be sustained by a smaller district.

Fig. 14[132] shows that the rural townships were modest in size ranging from 803 acres at Bowdon to 3679 acres at Hale (Hale appears smaller on the map because not all of old Hale falls within Trafford M.B.). Altrincham borough, carved out of Dunham Massey in 1290, was the smallest township at 657 acres.

The role of the Trafford townships was to provide water, arable land for communal strip farming, pasture, common meadow, woodland and waste (usually mossland, for rough grazing, peat, heather and fowl). Natural stream water could be supplemented by wells, easily dug through the sands and gravels. The rivers and smaller streams, acted as boundaries to townships, parishes and other administrative units.

The townships evolved during the Dark Ages, if not before. As well as townships containing nucleated early English (Anglo-Saxon) settlements, there were also townships in which settlements were mixed, possibly of Celtic, Saxon or Scandinavian origin particularly in north Trafford (such as Davyhulme, Danish in origin, close to Dumplington, Anglo-Saxon).

The townships contained many more farms by 1800 than are shown on the map because those inside the villages and in Altrincham and Stretford are too numerous to indicate.

In summary:
1. Each ancient township was a moderately sized irregular polygon.
2. Each township had a boundary on a river, apart from Altrincham and Timperley which shared a brook.
3. Township centres were nearer than a mile to a boundary stream.
4. Watling Street, streams, the Carr Ditch and mosses were used as boundaries.
5. By the end of the medieval period there were many water-powered corn mills, at least one per major township.
6. Dunham, Bowdon and Hale had castles in the early medieval period which later disappeared. All townships possessed one or more halls, several of which had declined to farms by 1800.
7. Not all townships possessed nucleated villages by 1800 (for example, Sale did not, nor the Trafford part of Barton).
8. Most villages had spawned hamlets; some developed at the edge of townships as bridgeheads into the wastes.
9. Farms also developed at the edges of townships where they, like some hamlets, served to define the bounds and be bases for expansion of settlement into the woods and moss commons between the townships. A ring pattern of farms developed round some mosses.

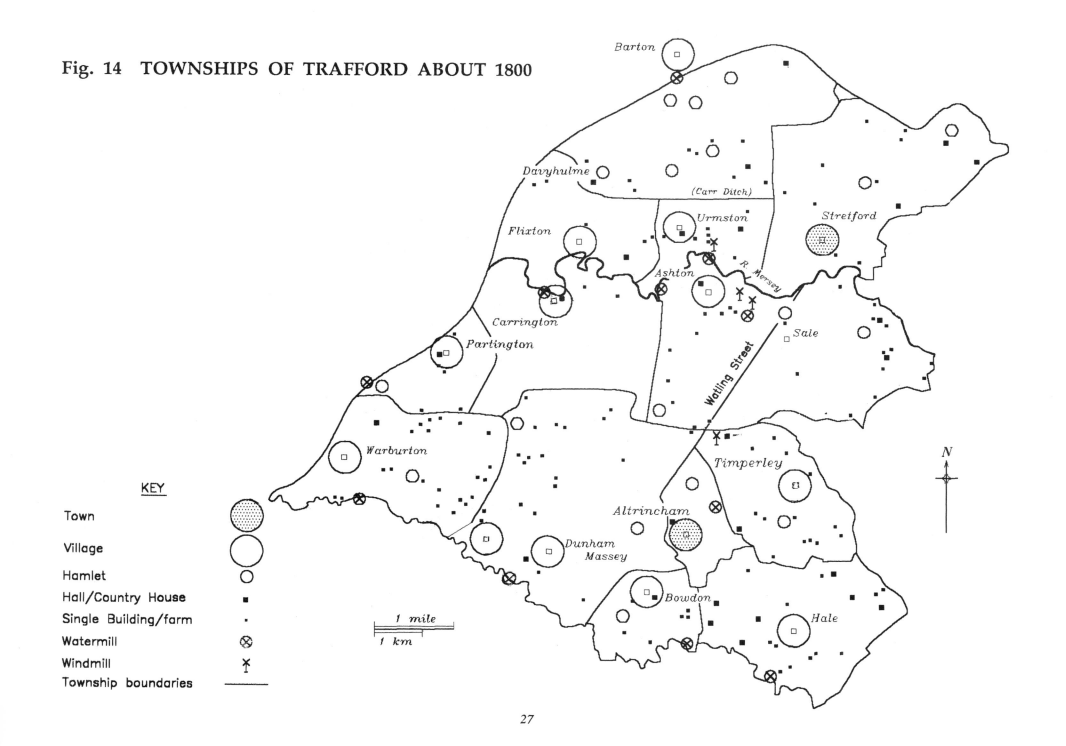

Fig. 14 TOWNSHIPS OF TRAFFORD ABOUT 1800

Barton

Davyhulme

(Carr Ditch)

Flixton

Urmston

Stretford

Ashton

R. Mersey

Carrington

Partington

Sale

Watling Street

Warburton

Timperley

KEY

Town

Village

Hamlet

Hall/Country House

Single Building/farm

Watermill

Windmill

Township boundaries

Altrincham

Dunham Massey

Bowdon

Hale

N

1 mile

1 km

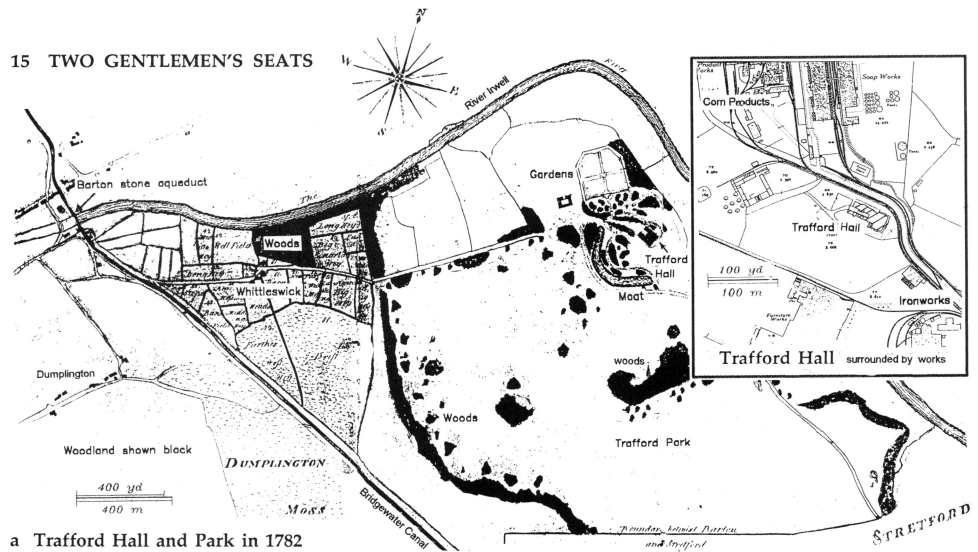

15 TWO GENTLEMEN'S SEATS

Barton stone aqueduct

Woods

Whittleswick

Dumplington

Woodland shown black

400 yd

400 m

DUMPLINGTON

Bridgewater Canal

Moss

River Irwell

Gardens

Trafford Hall

Moat

woods

Woods

Trafford Park

Boundary betwixt Barton and Stretford

STRETFORD

Corn Products

Soap Works

Trafford Hall

Ironworks

100 yd

100 m

Trafford Hall surrounded by works

a Trafford Hall and Park in 1782

Whittleswick Hall, later known as Trafford Hall, was acquired by the de Traffords in 1632. They lived originally at Trafford Old Hall by the Chester road near Cornbrook and moved to Whittleswick Hall in 1720,[133] possibly to escape the busy road and have an open environment where they could enjoy landscaped grounds. Whittleswick Hall had a park and this was extended several times. The map is an estate map of 1782, improved by hand for clarity. By 1782 some Whittleswick fields had been incorporated in the park. The hamlet of Whittleswick was demolished after this date for an extension of the park to 600 acres. The inset map shows the fate of the hall in the later industrialised park. It was surrounded by works, and a road and railway skirted it. After use as a hotel, golf club, prospective brewery, military hospital and billet, it was demolished just after World War II.[134]

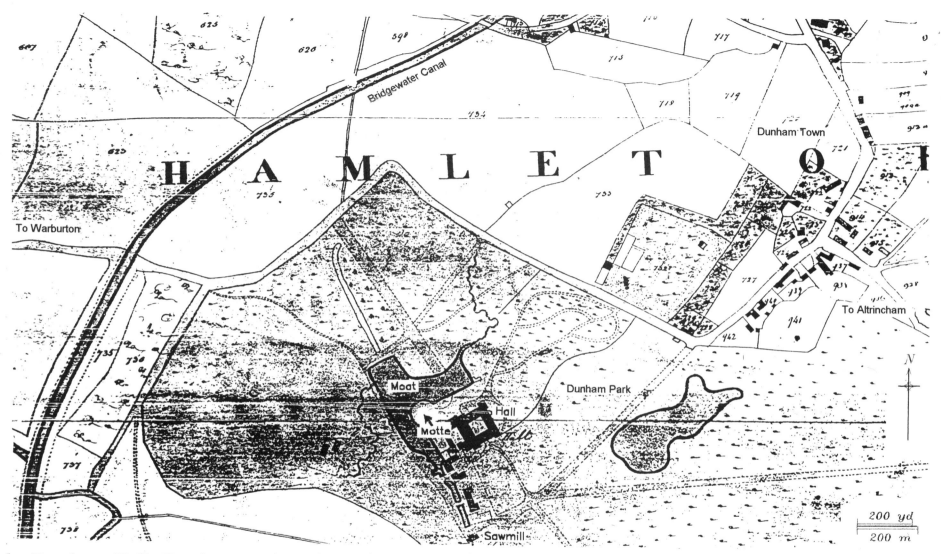

b Dunham Hall, Dunham Park and Dunham Town in 1841

The hall stood on the site of a medieval castle, the outline of its motte can be seen near the north-west corner. The hall was of sixteenth and early seventeenth century design with much alteration in the early eighteenth century.[135] A water cornmill, now a sawmill, survived from 1616 and the walled orchard was added later. The stables were built, courtyard rebuilt and park laid out in the early eighteenth century by George Booth, Earl of Warrington. Tenants had to provide 100,000 trees for planting.[136] Dunham Town, a T-junction village, 500m (1/3m) from the hall was probably once bigger. The shape of some fields suggests they were formerly divided into strips for communal farming. Some were cut through by the canal in 1765. The right-angled bend of the road to Warburton was probably due to land being taken to increase the size of the park.

16 TRAFFORD IN 1801

This is the first of four maps shown in this atlas derived from the censuses at fifty-year periods, 1801, 1851, 1901 and 1951. These dates are arbitrarily based on the decennial censuses and differ in quality of information because census practices changed. The format of the four maps is the same with the size of the total population being shown by proportionate-sized circles and the resulting circles divided into sections representing the proportions of the population in selected categories of work. **Fig. 16**, derived from the figures for 1801,[137] shows that total populations were generally quite low but that three places had over one thousand inhabitants: Altrincham (1692), Stretford (1477) and Flixton (1093). Stretford was already a small town and Flixton was twice the size of Urmston at that date. Elsewhere populations were small between 300 and 800. The total population was approximately 10,000.

Details of employment are also shown but these are very puzzling and certainly conflict with information from directories of the period. Three categories were listed for each township: i. persons chiefly employed in agriculture; ii. persons chiefly employed in trade, manufacture or handicrafts; iii. all other persons not comprised in the two previous classes. If we accept the census figures at face value, it seems it is a misconception to think that nineteenth century economic activity in Trafford was mainly agricultural. The map shows that in 1801 agriculture was dominant only in Ashton-on-Mersey, Bowdon, Sale, Stretford and Warburton. At Flixton and Urmston, trade and manufacture were dominant, especially hand-loom weaving. Activities (not specified) other than agriculture or trade and manufacture were dominant at Altrincham, which conflicts with directories detailing activities of a market town,[138] and were also dominant at Dunham and Timperley, which must have been clearly agricultural. It is not only difficult to identify the activities of the third category of 'all other persons...' listed by the census clerks but there seem to be serious differences in the various clerks' definition of who should be included in this category. It is clear the numbers occupied in the three categories at each place add up to the *total* population, not the *working* population. In other words, the figure for those not engaged in either 'agriculture' or 'manufacture, trade and handicrafts' in Altrincham, Carrington, Dunham, Flixton. Timperley and Urmston, *included all the housewives and children*. No wonder it contained a large section of the populace! This category would also include professional and personal services but except in Altrincham, these occupations would be minimal. However, at other places this category could not possibly contain all the wives and children: Ashton (13), Bowdon (4), Partington (7), Sale (8), Warburton (10), as well as Stretford (nil) show few (or no) persons 'not comprised in the two previous classes'; the low figures could not possibly represent wives and children, who must have been distributed among the other classes at these places.

Almost certainly employment was carried on in each local area. There is little evidence of commuting before the MSJ&A Railway of 1849 except for small scale daily movement by private carriage, canal boat or horse bus. This map shows that mapping statistics can sometimes be rather misleading and puzzling!

Fig. 16 POPULATION AND OCCUPATIONS 1801

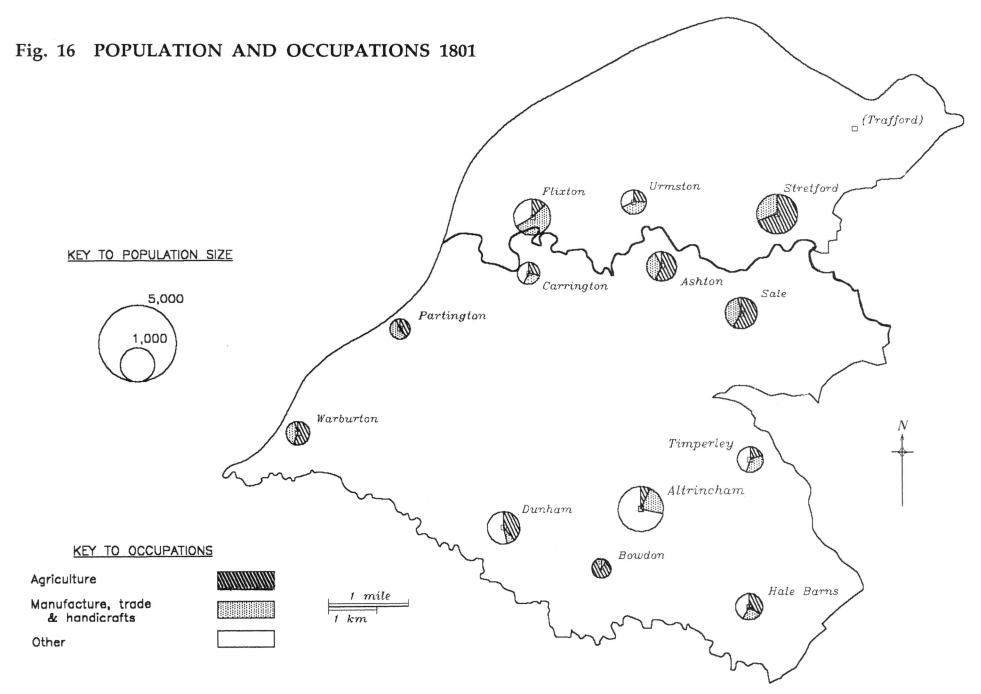

KEY TO POPULATION SIZE

5,000

1,000

KEY TO OCCUPATIONS

Agriculture

Manufacture, trade
& handicrafts

Other

1 mile

1 km

(Trafford)

Flixton

Urmston

Stretford

Carrington

Ashton

Sale

Partington

Warburton

Timperley

Altrincham

Dunham

Bowdon

Hale Barns

N

17 FEATURES OF THE RURAL LANDSCAPE BEFORE THE INDUSTRIAL PERIOD

Greens

Trafford is noteworthy for its numerous 'greens', sometimes associated with hamlets of the same name. These, shown schematically on **Fig. 17**, were often some distance from a village centre and were therefore not always conventional village greens[139] though those at Partington and Sale may have been exceptions. The others were probably where local animals were pastured. Mention has been made in Section 13 of the possibility that several bigger open spaces, shaped like irregular ovals (such as Trafford Old Park) might have been, before they became medieval parks, open arable areas or large ranges for herding animals together for transit out of the district. The greens might have been part of this pastoral system, supplying the major stock 'ovals' with local animals. Some greens were adjacent to the larger 'ovals'. Davenport Green, next to former Sunderland Park gave its name to that 'oval'. Dumplington Green was close to Trafford New Park, Sinderland Green to the Sinderland-Broadheath waste. In 1290 Hamon de Massey in his borough charter for Altrincham[140] allowed the burgesses "*common pasture and turbary of the heath within the boundaries of Dunham, Altrincham and Timperley, saving to myself and my heirs our improvements and ... the enclosure of Sinderland at our free will.*" This puts a date of the late thirteenth century on the possible beginnings of enclosure of open ranges and the emergence of Sinderland hamlet to farm the enclosed range and its green.

Ovals

The 'oval' areas, open spaces, here assumed to be used for the assembling of animals, were the 'old' and 'new' Trafford Park (**Figs. 13, 15a and 17**), Warburton Park (**Fig. 11**), Dunham Park (**Fig. 15b**) and Sunderland Park. It is possible this type of animal trade went on from ancient times to the pre-industrial period. At Domesday, the Sunderland oval was a manor shared by Hamon de Massey of Dunham and two other lords who probably used it for animals for their three demesnes. The 'tunstall' element of the name of the lost manor of Alretunstall near Sunderland was a term connected with animal husbandry.[141] It is probable that in the thirteenth century farm animals were cleared out of some of the ranges to make deer parks, for example at Dunham Park, Warburton Park and Sunderland Park.[142] That some roads in Trafford were drovers' roads has been suggested. Watling Street and the road from Warburton to Hale were such roads. Down Watling Street would come animals from Salford, via Whittleswick and Trafford old park. Farther south a road from the west crossed the Mersey by a ford at Hollins Green (Hollins is derived from 'holly', used for animal food). South-eastwards the road continued towards London. Arranged in a linear pattern along this route there were three 'ovals' which could have been used as animal collecting grounds. These were Warburton, Dunham and Sunderland parks which were linked to vast grazing areas by a network of tracks. The grazing areas were the mosses and heaths of Carrington, Warburton, Sinderland Broadheath, Hale, Bowdon, Timperley, Trafford, Flixton, Stretford, and the moors of Sale and Urmston.

Manors, halls and moated houses

A manor was a feudal landholding not a topographical or settlement feature. A township could contain one manor or part of one, or more than one. There was a basic pattern where a township contained one vill worked as one manor under one lord who had a hall. At Domesday, Dunham, Bowdon, Hale and 'Alretunstall' were probably of this type. However, Dunham was also the chief place of a barony and owned many other sub-manors in other townships, not only in its local barony of Dunham Massey but elsewhere in England. The single manor of Bowdon was divided after Domesday into two moieties (parts or halves of manors), one of which was given to Birkenhead Priory; the other moiety was divided into two parts and Bowdon Hall was located in one of them.[143] Warburton was held for two manors with a hall only on one, Sunderland and Baguley were two townships which were held as three manors but probably had only two halls. Ashton-on-Mersey consisted of two moieties, one belonging to the Boydells of Dodleston, one to the

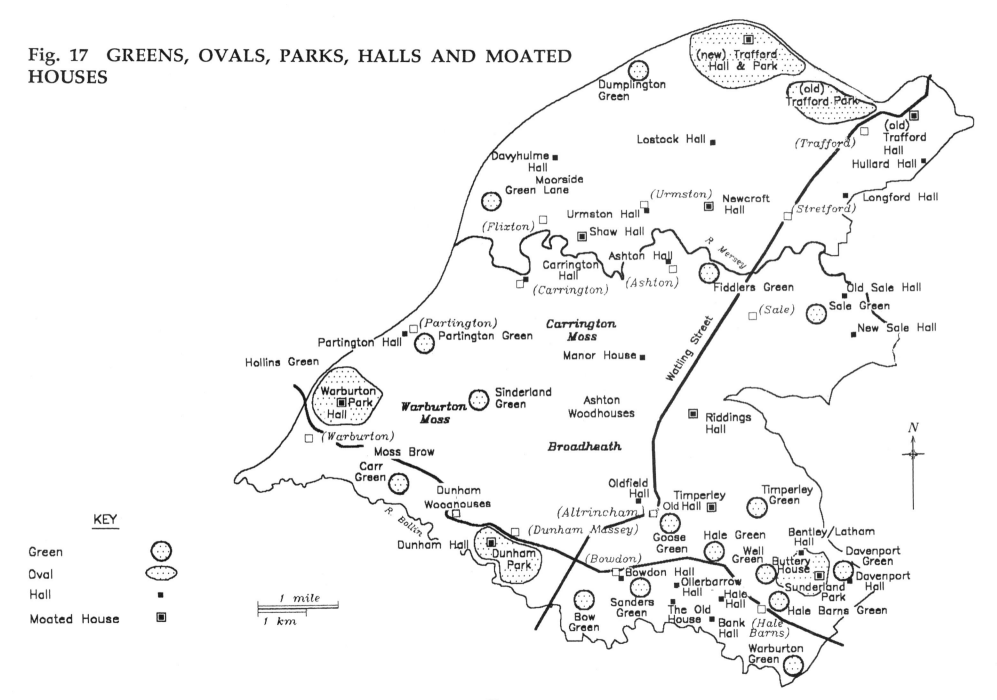

Fig. 17 GREENS, OVALS, PARKS, HALLS AND MOATED HOUSES

(new) Trafford Hall & Park

Dumplington Green

(old) Trafford Park

(Trafford)

(old) Trafford Hall

Lostock Hall

Hullard Hall

Davyhulme Hall

Moorside Green Lane

(Urmston)

Newcroft Hall

Longford Hall

Urmston Hall

(Stretford)

(Flixton)

Shaw Hall

Ashton Hall

R. Mersey

Carrington Hall

(Ashton)

Fiddlers Green

Old Sale Hall

(Carrington)

(Sale)

Sale Green

New Sale Hall

(Partington)

Carrington Moss

Partington Hall

Partington Green

Manor House

Watling Street

Hollins Green

Warburton Moss

Warburton Park Hall

Sinderland Green

Ashton Woodhouses

Riddings Hall

(Warburton)

Broadheath

Moss Brow

Carr Green

Oldfield Hall

Timperley Old Hall

Timperley Green

Dunham Woodhouses

(Altrincham)

Bentley/Latham Hall

N

R. Bollin

(Dunham Massey)

Goose Green

Hale Green

Well Green

Davenport Green

Dunham Hall

Dunham Park

(Bowdon)

Buttery House

Sunderland Park

Davenport Hall

KEY

Bowdon Hall

Ollerbarrow Hall

Hale Hall

Hale Barns Green

Green

Sanders Green

The Old House

Oval

Bow Green

Bank Hall

(Hale Barns)

Hall

1 mile

Moated House

1 km

Warburton Green

Carringtons[144] but there was a hall only on one. Timperley contained two moieties. One moiety had two halls, Old Hall and Riddings; the other moiety belonged to the Buckleys of Cheadle[145] and did not have a hall.

As new settlements were founded from existing ones, townships became sub-divided. Dunham is an instance where a township remained one manor but eventually had four sub-townships within it: Dunham Town, Dunham Woodhouses, Sinderland and Oldfield. Part of Oldfield was given to the borough of Altrincham[146] in 1290. There was an Oldfield Hall in the seventeenth century[147] but no evidence of an earlier one in that sub-township.

Hale was mentioned in Domesday Book (1086) as being one manor but its township enclosed the sub-manors of Sunderland and Alretunstall. At Domesday it had a 'rider', no doubt a military retainer who lived probably in his own hall on a separate estate, though the extent of this, or any sub-manor, is unknown. In 1342 Richard del Bonk (Bank) was mentioned in a document,[148] indicating that Bank Hall was already a residence though the extent of this possible sub-manor is unknown. Also a famous battling knight, Sir Thomas Danyers, owned much land (120 acres) in Hale at the same period but the location of a hall connected with him is unknown. Eventually, and remarkably, Hale had seven halls: Bank Hall, Bentley/Latham Hall, Buck Hall, Davenport Green Hall, Hale Hall, Ollerbarrow Hall and The Old House.[149]

Trafford had a number of moated sites.[150] Trafford Old Hall, Trafford New Hall, Buttery House Farm, Dunham Hall and Warburton Hall were in possible oval 'animal assembly' areas. Timperley Old Hall overlooked a large grazing area, Hale Moss. Moats would have prevented animals reaching the houses. They were fashionable and gave privacy and kudos to those who lived in houses protected by them.

Secondary villages, hamlets, decline of settlements, reclamation of the wastes, and enclosure of the commons

After the medieval period 'daughter' settlements developed, hamlets such as Crofts Bank and villages, such as Four Lane Ends (Timperley) and Dunham Woodhouses. On the other hand, some nucleated settlements may have declined into hamlets, for example, Sale where there were only two hamlets by 1801.[151]

Several places were bases for inroads into the wastes, see **Fig. 10** and show by their names the type of territory being colonised: Dunham 'Wood'houses, Ashton 'Wood'houses, Shaw (='wood'), 'Moss' Brow, Carr (='heath') Green, 'Moor'side. Carrington Moss was 'attacked' from several hamlets round it. Warburton Moss had Moss Brow nearby. Sinderland, Seamons and Timperley mosses were drained from Sinderland, Broadheath and Riddings; Annetts Moss at Stretford, from New Croft Hall. Enclosure depended on the whim of the landlord to initiate change. However, the powerful ratepayers of Altrincham were able to resist the Earl of Stamford's wish to enclose Hale Moss until 1880 when part of it became Stamford Park. Mention has been made that the support of Parliament was necessary to drain Trafford Moss in 1793 partly to increase the size of Trafford Park. Sale Moor was enclosed in 1806 and encircled by farms. Hamlets and farms are found around former 'ovals' when they were enclosed from medieval parks, such as Sunderland Park (Davenport Green). When the wetlands lost their value as providers of peat, fowl and rushes, they were enclosed. Villages, hamlets and farms were part of a system for extending the area of occupancy for the community.

Enclosures of the strips, doles or butts in the common arable, and of meadow, went on piecemeal from medieval times by agreement with the landlord. By 1700 there is little evidence for the communal working of openfield, the rotation of strips having ceased. Some enclosed and unenclosed strips remained but were held in severalty. Enclosure creating patch fields was more or less complete by 1800.[152] Enclosure was a pre-requisite for the spread of ring-fenced farms away from the village centres.

18 TYPES OF SETTLEMENTS BEFORE THE MID-NINETEENTH CENTURY

The types of settlements described below are illustrated by a number of map extracts. Small letters '(a)-(l)' refer to the maps in this section, 'Fig. x' to a map elsewhere in the atlas. Dates on the map titles refer to the publication or edition of a particular map. The evolution, spacing, shape and pattern of settlement groups, both large and small will be considered but not of individual buildings such as farms.

The evolution of places

The compact character of many places in Trafford stems mainly from a Saxon origin though small places like Lostock, Whittleswick, Dumplington and Bromyhurst suggest a continuation of scattered settlements possibly on Romano-British sites. The evolution[153] of places was as follows:

1. The first settlements were focii of agriculturally self-sufficient townships, requiring adequate water, arable, pasture and wasteland.

2. In medieval times five villages had developed and the borough of Altrincham was created. Subsidiary halls and sub-manors were founded in economically sound townships following the transfer of territory through, for example, an allocation of land given for military or other service; or property sold or given as dowry. In some places hamlets developed.

3. Foundation of farms outside the villages occurred after the Black Death in 1348 and Hundred Years War leading to the rise of yeomanry.

4. A decline of population led to a fall in the number and quality of houses until the sixteenth century.[154]

5. A second phase of farm building and a 'Great Rebuilding' of older properties in the seventeenth and eighteenth centuries followed the enclosure of openfields and wastes at the time of a further rise of yeomanry. There was some decline of villages and larger hamlets as some people moved out to outlying ring-fenced farms.

6. From the seventeenth to early nineteenth centuries new clusters developed at crossroads and along roads, for example, at Cross Street at Sale.

7. In the nineteenth century there was a last phase of farm foundation.

8. By 1800 there were two towns and eleven substantial villages.

Spacing

Subjective spatial analysis suggests that early agriculturally self-sufficient core settlements existed at about 2.2 miles intervals in farmable areas. As agricultural productivity increased, new small villages and hamlets filled the interstices at about a mile apart, and farms at about half a mile.

The shape of places

Three types of shape are identified here: *clustered* (compact villages or hamlets), *linear* (street settlements) and *scattered* places.

1. Places which were compact nuclear *clusters* of buildings: *Bowdon* (e); *Partington* (j); *Warburton* (Fig. 11); *Altrincham* (Fig. 12).

2a. Places which were *linear* in shape ('street settlements'): *Urmston* (f); *Ashton-on-Mersey* (g); *Carrington* (c); *Davyhulme* (Fig. 10); *Dunham Woodhouses* (Fig. 10); *Timperley (Green Head)* (b); *Hale (Barns)* (a); *Partington Millbank* (k); *Cross Street (Sale)* (Fig. 10); *Dumplington and Whittleswick* (i).

2b. Street settlements with a X-shaped plan, at *crossroads*: *Timperley (Four Lane Ends)* (Fig. 10); *Crofts Bank (Davyhulme)* (Fig. 10); *Stretford* (h).

2c. Street settlements with a T-shaped plan at a *T-junction – Dunham Town* (Fig. 15b); *Flixton* (Fig. 10).

3. *Scattered places*: small halls such as *Lostock* (**f**); *Riddings* (**d**) and *Hullard* (**Fig. 17**) and hamlets such as *Bromyhurst* (**i**) (*and farms*).

Assuming most places started as small clusters, as time went on most became street settlements which shows the influence of communications on shape. Two clustered ones, *Warburton* and *Partington* lay isolated on the outer periphery of Trafford and were perhaps isolated from the development of roads. Many scattered places were probably daughter settlements from existing places, founded sometimes near former mosses when they were drained.

The pattern of the constituent parts within townships in Trafford

1. Sizeable places with an integral or adjacent hall: *Bowdon* (**e**); *Carrington* (**c**); *Partington* (**j** and **k**); *Ashton-on-Mersey* (**g**).

2. Place with a hall and another separate from it: *Urmston* (**f**).

3. Places with no integral hall but with hall(s) some distance away: *Dunham* (**Fig. 15b**); *Warburton* (**Fig. 11**); *Hale* (*Barns*) (**a**); *Timperley* (**b** and **d**); *Stretford* (**h**) (Hullard Hall and Longford Hall, **Fig. 14**), *Trafford Old Hall* (**Fig. 15**); *Altrincham* (**Fig. 12**); *Flixton* (**Fig. 14**).

4. Townships with halls but with no significant settlement centre by the early nineteenth century: *Sale (New and Old Halls)* (**l**); *Whittleswick (Trafford New Hall*, **Fig. 15a**); *Davyhulme* (**Fig. 14**); *Lostock Hall* (**f**).

5. Small townships with no hall: *Dumplington and Bromyhurst* (**i**).

Examples of early settlement patterns
a **Hale**[155] was the wealthiest manor at Domesday and therefore probably had a small nucleated settlement, assumed in this atlas to be on the site of Hale Barns. Later it had seven halls as already described. The later street village was situated at the highest point of Trafford attenuated along the ridgeway (A538) with stripfields round it.[156] Apart from a string of farms and halls along the road, other settlements occupied two zones roughly parallel to this, one along the north bank of the Bollin, the other along the valley of the Timperley Brook.

b **Timperley**[157] is shown as Green Head (a street village on Wood Lane), a location favoured by Pryor partly on evidence of the remains of strip fields in this area. On the tithe map of 1835 the present Timperley village was called Four Lane Ends, not shown here. Green Head was about 300 metres from Timperley Old Hall. An archaeological level at the hall site showed a date of 840AD. The hall, the home of the Masseys of Timperley in the medieval period, lay in the middle of the moated site. It was replaced by farms, including the one now the hotel north-west of the moat.

c **Carrington**[158] was a street village following the curved bank of the Mersey. The hall, the home of the Carrington family, lay between two separate halves of the village (the eastern end is not shown here). The hall though ancient never had a park. To the west lay a circular mill dam and mill surrounded by farms. The arable lands lay to the south and beyond them, Carrington Moss. Most of the village has disappeared and the hall area is a playground. Carrington is now industrial; on the south side of the road is a huge chemical works while to the north-west off the map was a coal-fired power station now decommissioned. (The map of late date was selected for its clarity.)

d **Riddings Hall**[159] a moated hall at the north end of Timperley Moss was isolated from any nuclear settlements. It was the home of the Ardernes and Vaudreys, and lay in a half-manor of Timperley. It was founded probably about 1475 after an agreement by three local lords to drain the moss in the valley of the Timperley Brook. The hall obtained one quarter of the moss. The straight and wide enclosures on the former moss to the south (right) are typical field shapes for drained land. The area was engulfed by suburban building post-World War I.

Fig. 18 SETTLEMENT PATTERNS

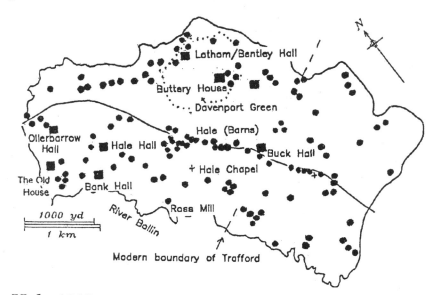

a Hale 1842 Halls and farms occupied three distinct zones.

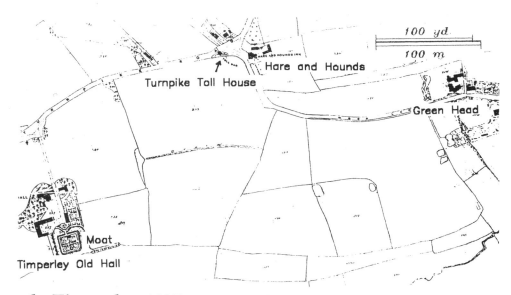

b Timperley 1835 Timperley Old Hall and Green Head, possibly the original village.

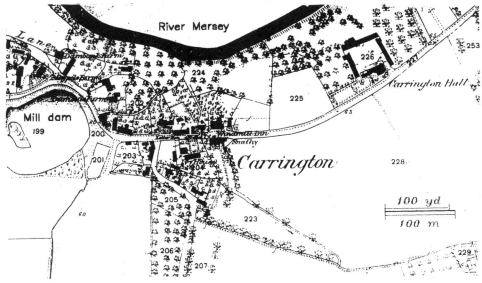

c Carrington 1876 The main village was around a mill west of the hall complex. Other houses lay to the east (right) off the map.

d Riddings Hall, Timperley 1835 The straight strip fields were reclaimed from Timperley Moss, south (right) of the hall.

e **Bowdon**[160] was mentioned at Domesday with a church and a priest. It had a huge parish extending north to the Mersey and it included some places now outside Trafford. Its sub-circular churchyard suggests there might have been a Celtic church here before Saxon times exercising religious control over a wide area comparable to that of Eccles. The village was a cluster of farms and houses round the church and lay on the ridgeway like Hale. The original single Domesday manor was divided into two moieties after the Conquest, one being given to Birkenhead Priory in 1150 (and eventually to Bowdon church). One half of the other moiety was given to the family which took its name from Bowdon. Their hall was built at the edge of the village and its occupants for some time were in administrative service to the incumbents of Dunham Hall. The run of the fields round the village suggests they were formerly divided in narrow strips, part of an openfield system.

f **Urmston,**[161] a manor of Barton, can be regarded as two broadly parallel street villages separated by orchards and closes, or one village with a big 'hole' in the middle of it. The two roads run east-west as do many roads in north Trafford such as Davyhulme road from the crossroad hamlet of Crofts Bank (just discernible top left) leading east past Lostock Hall, a sub-manor which was isolated from any nuclear settlement. Several boundaries run east-west such as the Carr or Nico Ditch. The ditch has been a boundary for centuries. Different field patterns on each side of it reflect the land belongs to different townships. As there was no soil difference to account for the distinction in field shapes, they must result from human decision making. The long thin fields tell us there was much openfield strip agriculture in former times. New Croft Hall, some distance from the village, was a medieval foundation in part concerned with draining part of Annett's Moss (not shown), most of which was in adjacent Stretford township.

g **Ashton-on-Mersey**[162] was a street village along a spur of fluvio-glacial sands and gravels leading towards a ford across the river to Urmston. The hall and church lay at the northern end of the village, virtually a dead end as far as modern communications are concerned. The manor was held in two moieties, one part by the Carringtons and the other by the Ashtons by military service from the Boydells. St Martins had incumbents from 1305.

h **Stretford**[163] ('Streetford') lay on the north bank of the wide Mersey floodplain where routes from north Trafford joined to cross the river southwards. As well as a river crossing, it was a crossroad settlement where west-east routes along Edge Lane and King Street, along the north bank of the Mersey valley, crossed Watling Street. Though the early settlement lay mainly on Watling Street, the street plan within the later town was triangular in shape. The map does not show any extension to the town because of the building of the Bridgewater Canal but there were wharves which increased the prosperity of the place in the late eighteenth century. Stretford belonged to Dunham till 1250 and then to the de Traffords. St Matthews was an early foundation, around 1413, as a chapel-of-ease to the collegiate church of Manchester in which parish it stood.

Fig. 18 SETTLEMENT PATTERNS – continued

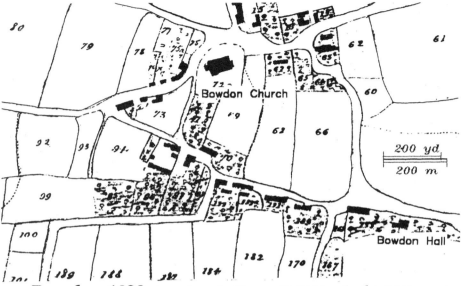

e Bowdon 1838 A nucleated village with St Mary's, the most ancient church foundation in Trafford and a hall adjacent to the village.

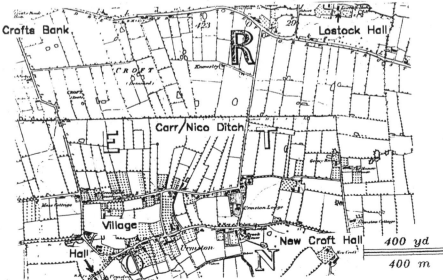

f Urmston 1848 An open-centred village with a hall. Lostock, a sub-manor of Barton, had a hall but no village. The Carr Ditch had been a boundary for centuries. Note how field patterns changed across it.

g Ashton-on-Mersey 1845 A street village leading to an ancient river crossing. The hall of 1810 lies on the site of a more ancient one.

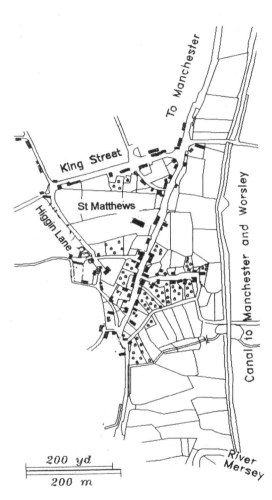

h Stretford 1782 A bridge settlement of triangular shape. King Street was part of an east-west route along the north bank of the river Mersey.

39

i **Dumplington and Whittleswick**[164] were two small street hamlets divided after 1761 by the Bridgewater Canal. Bromyhurst hamlet was nearby. Because the map was part of one sheet of an atlas of the Trafford estates, the fields of Whittleswick were not shown on this particular sheet but they can be seen on another map, **Fig. 15a**. The demise of Whittleswick occurred when its lands became part of an extension to Trafford (New) Park after 1782. The demise of Dumplington happened more recently when many of its fields were covered by The Trafford Centre. By 1782 all fields were enclosed except Dumplington Moss (bottom right) but the field name Dumplington Field above the inserted hamlet name 'Dumplington', though only of a single strip suggests that there was once a larger Dumplington Field and that the small hamlet worked a single open townfield. By the eighteenth century the strips had been enclosed into square-shaped fields. The long rectangular fields south of the settlement were probably enclosures from a once larger Dumplington Moss. This is reinforced by the fact that several fields to the west of Dumplington Moss carried the name 'moor' or 'moss'. Their alignments probably followed drainage channels.

j **Partington**,[165] like Carrington (c), lay on the flat, narrow bank of the Mersey on fertile glacial sands and gravels. Immediately south was Carrington Moss. Like Carrington, Partington was almost two villages, one of which lay to the north and contained the hall, the other lay to the south, separated from the hall group by an open space, Hall Croft, probably an early green. The village's openfields lay to the west and east of the hall cluster and still showed some narrow strips at the time of the tithe in 1835. Part of the western field was orchard by the date of the map shown here. In the northeast the fields by the railway (top right) were also in strips on the tithe map. The rectangular fields to the south were enclosures from the moss, possibly made by the people at Erlam Farm (under the large 'T'). A road ran westward to the hamlet of Millbank.

k **Partington Millbank**[166] was a linear hamlet along the Mersey bank. Immediately south was the boundary with Warburton. It was an industrial hamlet which may have had an ancient origin as a corn mill site, worked by water wheels, but in the late eighteenth century was first a paper works, then a corn mill again, then a metal slitting mill and finally once more a paper mill again, all before 1800. It had the first steam engine in Trafford in 1792 and continued as a paper works until the early twentieth century. This was a mirror image of a similar paper works site in Old Trafford – Throstle Nest mill in north Trafford. All the buildings of Millbank have disappeared.

l **Sale**.[167] This is a redraft of part of a map, which was difficult to decipher, of the estate of George Legh. With the site of Sale New Hall added it indicates that Sale at this date was not a village on School Road but two separate halls, with a scattered hamlet to the west, another at Cross Street, not shown, and a few farms. It may be there had been a nucleated village in ancient times which had disappeared. The name Legh reminds us that Sale manor was two moieties in the late medieval period, one held by the Masseys of Sale and the other by the Legh family of Warburton and Arley. The map is of part of the Arley moiety of the manor. Both halls have disappeared. Sale Moor today lies 2 or 3 kilometres (a mile and a half) to the east, off the map. It is curious how the name of the moor (enclosed in 1806) has shifted because it formerly extended westwards as far as Washway Road.

In conclusion, apart from the towns of Altrincham and Stretford, the most common nuclear rural settlement by the mid-nineteenth century was a street village with a hall at some distance. There was also a dense scatter of isolated halls, hamlets and farms. The south possessed most clustered places which suggests Saxon influence was strongest there. The north was characterised by street settlements and scattered places which suggests possibly some continuation of Scandinavian or Celtic settlement patterns in the former sphere of influence of Eccles.

Fig. 18 SETTLEMENT PATTERNS – continued

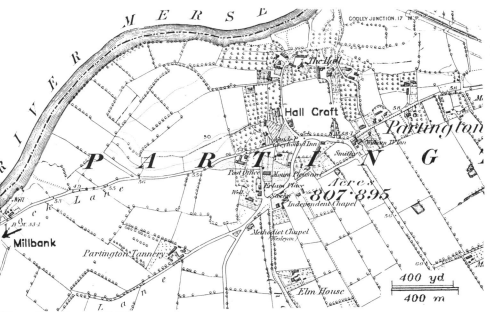

i Dumplington and Whittleswick 1782 Demise of two hamlets. The fields of Dumplington lie under the Trafford Centre. Whittleswick vanished when Trafford Park was extended in the early 19c.

j Partington 1881 There were three parts: the hall complex, the T-junction village and Millbank industrial hamlet.

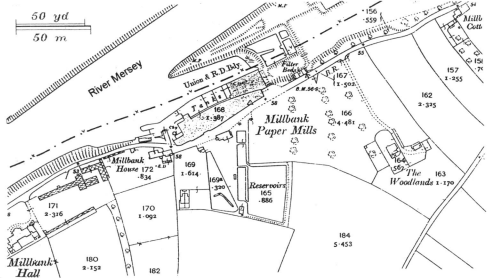

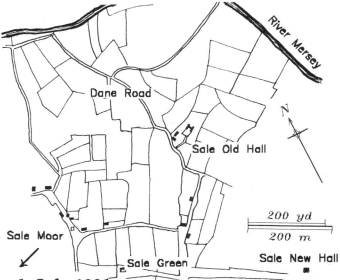

k Partington Millbank 1881 Demise of a hamlet. The paper industry started on a corn mill site on the Mersey (now the Manchester Ship Canal). All the buildings have gone.

l Sale 1801 Redraft of a map of the estate of George Legh. The site of the New Hall has been added. Sale Moor lay south-west of Sale, not south-east as now.

19   TRAFFORD IN 1851

The power of the major landowners continued through their policies towards canals and, later, railways, in their interference in local government (such as that by the Stamfords),[168] in their control of farming, in their control of the release of land for residential building[169] and industrial premises, for example, in north Trafford,[170] and in requiring tight standards of building construction, for example, in south Trafford.[171] Socially there was a great gap to the next bands of landowners, for example, from the Stamfords to the Brooks and Harrops[172] and so to the small landowners. It was on land sold by the last group (at least in south Trafford) that early mass housing was built.[173] As land was taken from farming, it was frequently turned over first to market gardening[174] then to building. Enclosure of moss and moor continued, for example, of Sale Moor for farming, 1806.[175]

As places grew rapidly in population new public buildings appeared concerned with a new type of administration by local boards, using, in the case of Altrincham a former residence for offices and a new town hall built in 1849[176] adjacent to the Unicorn. Shops and offices displaced what had been agriculturists' dwellings. Between the 1801 and 1851 censuses several small places declined; for example, Flixton 1821-51, Partington 1831-41, Urmston and Carrington 1841-51 and Warburton 1831-51 all lost population due to agricultural depression and emigration into industrial and urban areas for work (census comments). Nevertheless, by 1851, **Fig. 19**,[177] the population of Trafford had doubled to approximately 21000. Stretford, 4998 persons, had passed Altrincham in size. Bowdon, Timperley and Hale were increasing modestly, though the railway had hardly affected the first two and had not yet arrived at Hale. The statistics regarding occupation do not have the clarity of the 1801 census because details were provided not for individual townships but for extensive Registration Districts. The two districts concerned were Altrincham District (including south Trafford but extending farther south) and Barton-on-Irwell District (including north Trafford but extending farther north). There were twice as many employed in agriculturally-related industries in Altrincham District compared with Barton and twice the proportion employed in trade and manufactures (and extractive industries) in Barton compared with Altrincham (actually most of the manufacturing and extractive industry, coalmining, was in that part of the Barton district north of the Irwell). The textile factory industry of Flixton (Stott's 1851, see Langton) and the paper making of Throstle Nest were mirrored south of the Mersey by the textile factories of Altrincham and paper mills at Partington. Proportions in retail trade, labouring, service industries and professions were about the same and this similarity of the Barton area with the places in Altrincham district is interesting.

In 1849 the MSJ&AR line had reached Altrincham where there had been small-scale commuting for some decades by private carriage, canal boat and horse bus, and it was known as a residential town with many independents and servants. In fact in 1841 the largest occupied class in Altrincham was that of domestic servants.[178] After 1849 the Altrincham area, Stretford and other places on or near the line, were beginning massive growth as residential and commuting areas.

Fig. 19 POPULATION AND OCCUPATIONS 1851

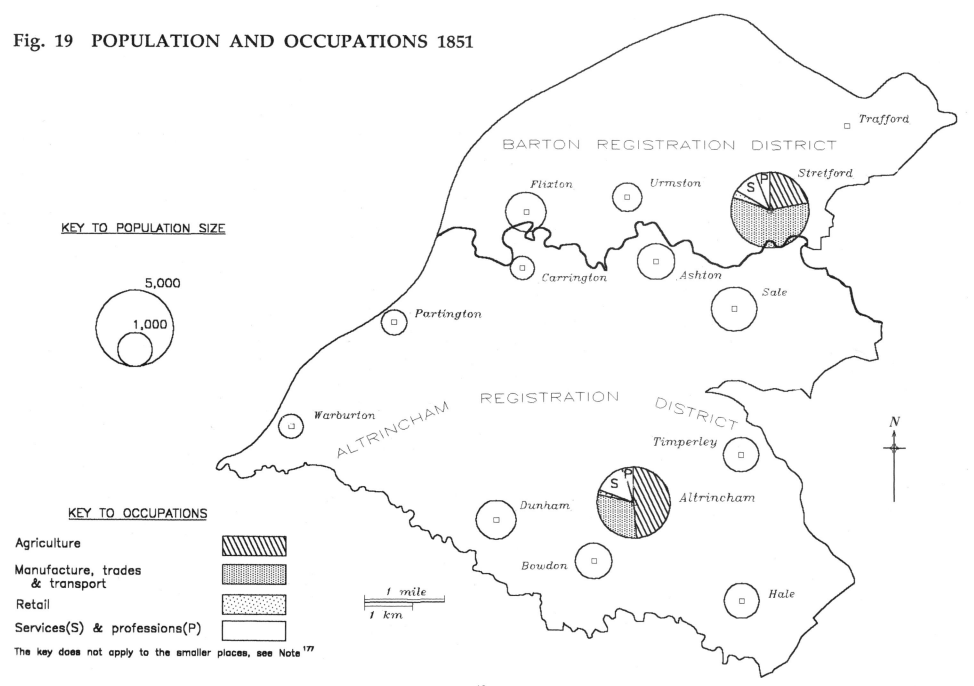

KEY TO POPULATION SIZE

5,000

1,000

KEY TO OCCUPATIONS

Agriculture

Manufacture, trades
  & transport

Retail

Services(S) & professions(P)

The key does not apply to the smaller places, see Note [177]

BARTON REGISTRATION DISTRICT

Trafford

Stretford

Flixton

Urmston

Carrington

Ashton

Sale

Partington

Warburton

ALTRINCHAM REGISTRATION DISTRICT

Timperley

Dunham

Altrincham

Bowdon

Hale

N

1 mile

1 km

Fig. 20 is a composite map of parts of Lancashire and Cheshire taken from the Ordnance Survey 1:63360, 'one inch to one mile' maps,[179] here reduced to fit the page. There are some later railways shown but these were added by the O.S. on old editions of the maps to avoid resurveying and so save costs! Though of the same general period as Fig. 19 this map contrasts with the previous one by showing details of the landscape. There is no clear indication of height because on this reproduction the shading (hachures) was restricted to the south-east corner and has not reproduced. The meandering Irwell and Mersey are shown well. The Irwell-lower Mersey could be crossed by bridges at Old Trafford, Barton and Davyhulme (there was no bridge indicated at Warburton) and by ferries at Irlam and Hollins. All the chief mosses and moors were still in existence though the small Annetts Moss and Seamons Moss were not indicated, presumably reclaimed. Carrington Moss was still vast.

The map seems really 'busy' with dozens of small roads which reflects the interest in communications at the time and indicates the essentially rural nature of most of Trafford. If the network of lines of roads is related to the amount of agricultural or other activity in an area, the most 'active' areas were: i. Old Trafford; ii. a belt from Davyhulme to Lostock; iii. two zones, one on each side of the Mersey, i.e. a belt from Moorside, via Flixton and Urmston to Stretford and another from Partington via Carrington and Ashton to Sale; iv. a narrow band along the Sinderland Brook from Millbank to Timperley; v. a zone south of the Bridgewater Canal from Dunham Woodhouses through Oldfield, Altrincham and Bowdon to Timperley.

Trafford Park and Dunham Park stood out as major estates at opposite ends of Trafford. Apart from Dunham Hall and Trafford 'House', other halls were at Davyhulme, Shaw, Urmston, New Croft, Hullard, Longford, Partington, Carrington, Ashton, Sale New and Old, Woodheys, Riddings, Timperley, Oldfield, Bowdon, Davenport Green, and Bank. Warburton Hall and several Hale halls were not named.

Whether this was at the whim of the cartographer or if they had become lesser farms is not known. In the north the buildings of Manchester and Old Trafford were contiguous, Old Trafford was now virtually an extension of the built-up area of Manchester. Elsewhere the chief places were still separated but houses were being built along the roads between them, for example, from Hulme Bridge over the Irwell (Davyhulme) and from Barton on the old turnpike through Lostock to Stretford; from Irlam Ferry through Flixton and Urmston to Stretford; from Crossford Bridge to Woodheys; from Ashton-on-Mersey through 'new Sale' to old Sale on Dane Road; and from Timperley to Altrincham. Hamlets had appeared at Crofts Bank and Woods End near Davyhulme, at Gorsey Brow near Urmston, at Old Trafford, at Cross Street (Sale), at New Chester and Woodheys on the Chester road turnpike, at Booth Hey near Carrington, at Broad Oak near Sinderland, at Birch House near Ashton Woodhouses, at Peel Causeway at Hale, at Warburton Green, from the Hare and Hounds corner along to Timperley on the Stockport turnpike, and on Moss Lane and Deansgate Lane. Most of these were linear settlements along existing roads. Along the Bridgewater Canal small groups of buildings could be found at Barton, Cornbrook, Watersmeet, Stretford, Dane Road, Sale (near 'Sale Moor' station), Deansgate Lane, Broadheath, Seamons Moss Bridge (Lower Houses) and at the north end of Dunham Town.

The intricate pattern of small roads and turnpikes together with that of the canal system gives a good idea of a busy Trafford in the horse age.

Fig. 20 A LAST VIEW OF PRE-INDUSTRIAL TRAFFORD

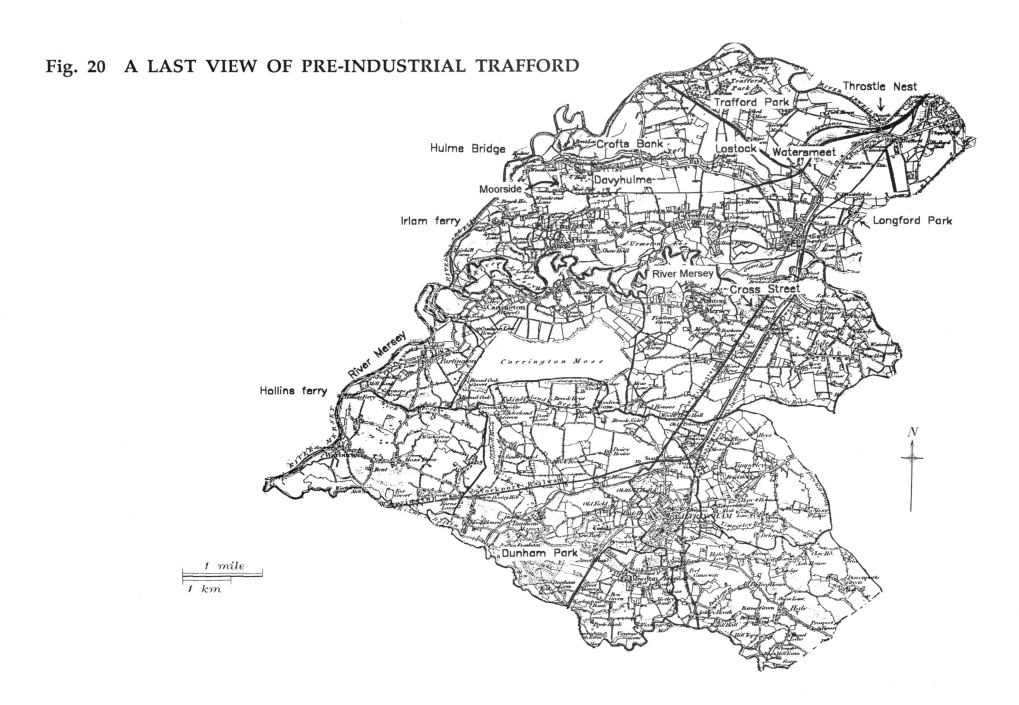

21 TRAFFORD IN 1901

Trafford had experienced two major explosions in the nineteenth century. The first was a tremendous growth of population. Trafford in 1901 had grown massively, more than fourfold from 1851 and tenfold from 1801 to about 94,000 of which Stretford had one third (30,436), Fig. 21.[180] Stretford had grown sixfold in fifty years, twenty times over the century. Its remarkable growth was mainly from the massive development of housing for people working mainly in Manchester, or at places in the recently built Manchester Ship Canal system, 1894, or in Trafford Park opened for industry in 1896. Altrincham (16,831) had grown fourfold from 1851, but only to little over half that of Stretford. Most of the small textile factory industries near the town centre had gone but it was now supported by the development of the Broadheath industrial area from the 1880s and by its increasing role as a residence for commuters. Sale was not far behind with 12,088 persons. The chief commuting practices were by walking, bicycles, horse buses, the MSJ&A Railway and Cheshire Lines Railways (north Cheshire and Urmston areas).

The railways occupied much space with their lines and buildings but another feature affected the urban skyline. Accompanying the explosion in population and the spread of housing, a second explosion produced a rapid increase in the number of churches and chapels. Whereas there had been a handful of churches and parishes a century before, by 1901 two dozen more had been founded and many chapels. Another vast increase was in the number of inns, hotels and beerhouses.

It might be thought that the rise, by 1901, of Stretford above that of Altrincham (the ancient urban centre) and the rapid rise also of Sale, that population in places in Trafford became relatively lower with increasing distance from Manchester. Certainly there is little doubt that north Trafford was now an appendage to Manchester, part industrial, part commuting. However, in 1901, Urmston 6,594, Flixton 3,656, Timperley 3,215, Davyhulme 1,231, Carrington 514 and Partington with 587 were all nearer to Manchester than Altrincham but lower in population. Therefore, the likely geographical explanation seems to have been whether a place was in, or not in, the tripartite eastern spine of communications: the A56, the Bridgewater Canal and MSJ&A Railway. The old contrast between north and south in Trafford was giving way to that between east and west, between places in the communications corridor which grew, and those off it, which did not.

Details of occupation were given in the census for places over 5,000 population, hence information for every place is not shown. Also details given varied from county to county, for example, details for agriculture were not given for places in north Trafford because of a different system of statistics used in Lancashire than in Cheshire; it is most probable that some agriculture was carried on in Stretford and Urmston. Hence the categories differ from those shown on Fig. 19. It is also difficult to equate the census categories with those of 1851 because the figures for that year were only for two registration districts. It is probably correct to infer that there had been a massive reduction in the proportion of people employed in agriculture in south Trafford as a whole, and a general increase in manufacturing, trade, transport and services ('Trade, etc.') in north Trafford. The 'empty' circles of Bowdon, Carrington, Dunham, Flixton, Hale, Partington, Timperley, Warburton show only the size of the populations, not the occupations of 'Trade, etc.' which are shown blank in the key.

The increase in manufacturing in the south was mainly due to the rise of Broadheath machine-tool manufacturing from the mid-1880s[181] and that in the north to Trafford Park's heavy industry from the 1890s but there was also a vast increase of smaller manufacturing in chemicals, dyes and paints and making parts for the rail-, horse- and boat-based economy, with smiths, farriers, wagon builders, ship and boat builders and repairers. The rise in trade occurred with improvements in storage, circulation of goods, and office systems and the spread of banking. The rise in transport came about because of the growth of railway systems including massive goods sidings, public horse transport systems and road and bridge construction. The increase in services was from the development of water supply and drainage facilities, gasworks, and in the last quarter of the nineteenth century, electric power stations. With the rise of wealth due to industry and trade there was a great increase of professional, public and personal services.

Fig. 21 POPULATION AND OCCUPATIONS 1901

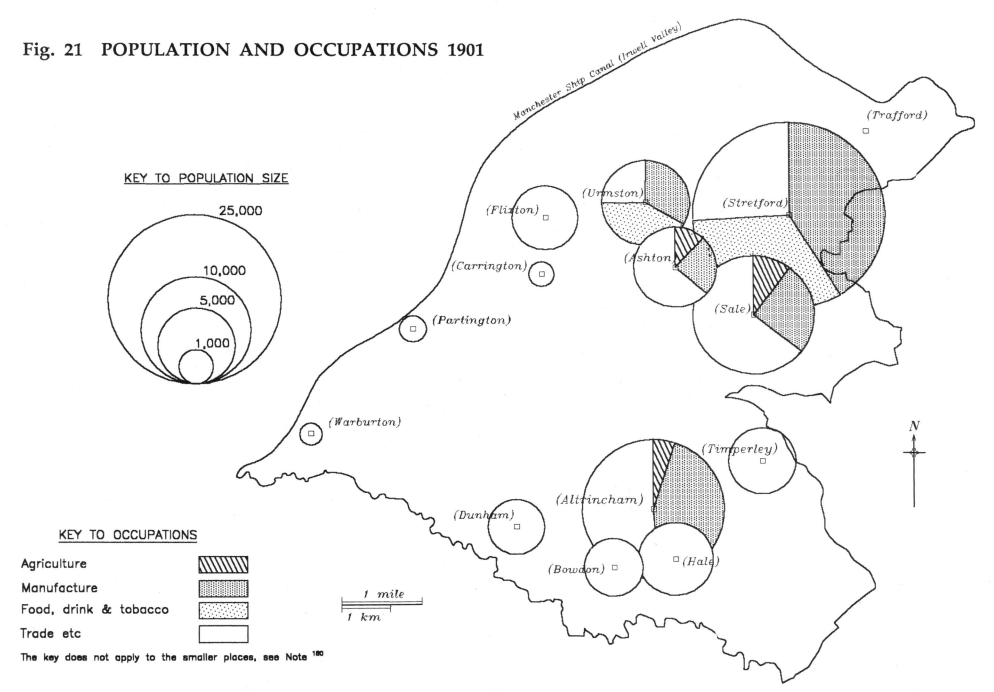

KEY TO POPULATION SIZE

25,000

10,000

5,000

1,000

Manchester Ship Canal (Irwell Valley)

(Trafford)

(Flixton)

(Urmston)

(Stretford)

(Carrington)

(Ashton)

(Sale)

(Partington)

(Warburton)

(Timperley)

(Altrincham)

(Dunham)

(Bowdon)

(Hale)

N

KEY TO OCCUPATIONS

Agriculture

Manufacture

Food, drink & tobacco

Trade etc

The key does not apply to the smaller places, see Note [180]

1 mile

1 km

22 COMMUNICATIONS FROM THE EIGHTEENTH CENTURY

Roads

The line of the earliest main road through Trafford, Watling Street, was Roman in origin. Used through the centuries, it was in poor condition by the time of the Industrial Revolution. It was one of three major road routes early turnpiked, **Fig. 22a**.[182] The first was along what is now the A56, linking Manchester and north Cheshire. The stretch from Altrincham southward was the earliest, 1752, while that further north was turnpiked in 1765, significantly the year when the Bridgewater Canal was opened, to which the directors of the trust hoped to offer competition. Second, there was a transverse rib from Chorlton to Barton, 1811, via a bridge across the Irwell, third, there was a link from Stockport to Altrincham, 1821; these two were a result of increase of traffic due to the industrialisation of places outside Trafford. The ancient importance of the Hale to Warburton road had faded. Before the railways were built, several stage and mail coach road routes ran through Trafford from Manchester to north Cheshire served by hostelries such as the Pelican in west Timperley and those round the market place in Altrincham.[183] That the B6211 was a turnpike but never became an A-road reflects the decline of importance of this route paralleling the Bridgewater Canal along which trade also declined. However, this road was eventually to be one of the few routes into industrial Trafford Park. The number of turnpikes down the eastern side of Trafford shows the importance of travel and trade along the eastern corridor between the mid-eighteenth and early nineteenth centuries.

After canals and railways were built a fan pattern of feeder roads developed to some of the bridges, canal wharves and stations, leading to ribbon residential development along them. Examples are: at Sale (Broad Road and Hope Road), at Brooklands (Brooklands Road and Hope Road), at Navigation Road (Wellington Road and Brook Lane), at Altrincham (Barrington Road, Ashley Road and Oxford Road) at Hale (Victoria Road, Broomfield Lane and Cecil Road). This did not occur in the Urmston area which retained its ancient rectangular pattern of roads.

Canals

The Bridgewater Canal was built from Worsley to reach markets for the Duke of Bridgewater's coal from Worsley. It was started in 1761 and passed through north Trafford to Manchester a year later. Various routes had been considered but when the pattern made by the final choice on **Fig. 22b** is examined this was a curiously indirect route from Worsley to Manchester. Instead of travelling almost due east from Worsley, the canal struck south-eastwards across the Irwell to Old Trafford to a point 5 kilometres (three miles) southwest of Manchester and then had to make a huge dog-leg turn north-eastwards to Manchester. This route was to avoid the cost of making the channel through Salford by taking a cheaper course across Trafford Moss. Having to circumnavigate the de Trafford family's estate of Trafford (New) Park, 1720, affected the route of an undertaking in the eighteenth century equivalent to diverting a motorway today. There followed the inspiration to create a junction at Watersmeet to tap the trade of north Cheshire and the canal was built through the rest of Trafford by 1765. It was a happy coincidence that by following the 83 feet contour to avoid building locks, the canal ran adjacent to Watling Street and served Stretford and Altrincham before being deflected westwards by the Altrincham ridge. In avoiding higher land the canal skirted the (lower) ridge of Dunham Massey and its park. Late eighteenth century maps do not show a sudden increase of settlement building activity caused by the canal. This did not occur until the early nineteenth century. The importance of the Bridgewater Canal increased to a high point by the 1840s[184] but was then suddenly diminished by transfer of some goods and all passengers to the MSJ&AR after 1849; Lord Egerton of Tatton, who owned the canal land, was given shares in the railway on condition he withdrew his passenger boats. The canal had created the port-hamlet of Broadheath, a small boat building industry at Stretford, some expansion of commercial activity at wharves at Stretford and Sale, and passenger and goods traffic to Manchester. The vegetable-growing industry of late eighteenth

Fig. 22 COMMUNICATIONS

a Main Roads

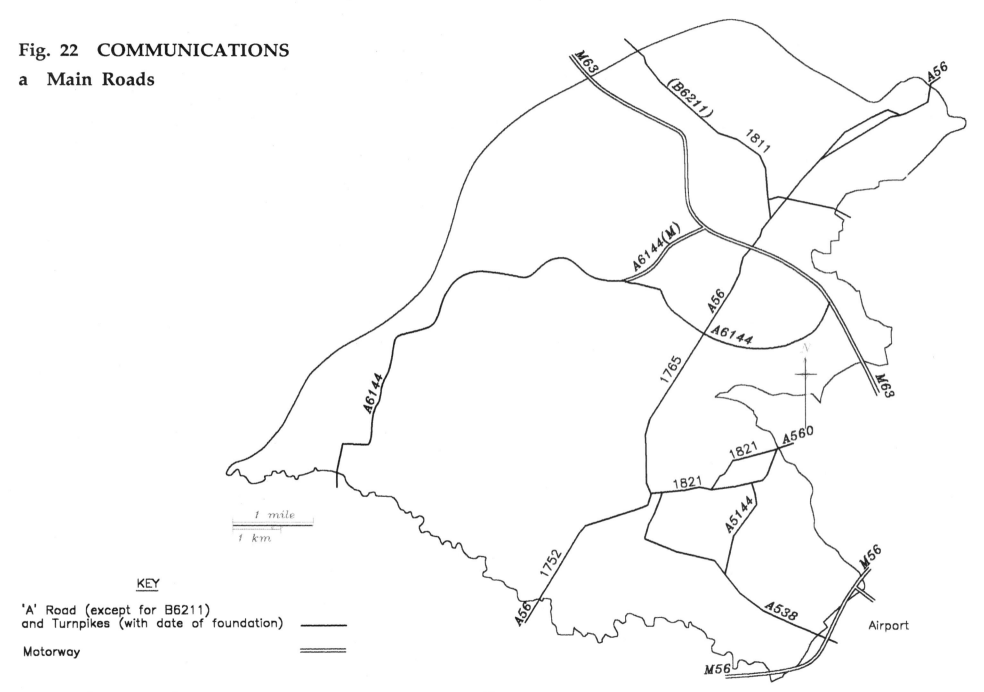

KEY

'A' Road (except for B6211)
and Turnpikes (with date of foundation) ————

Motorway   ══════

century Altrincham was dependent on nightsoil brought by barges. Trade continued until the mid-twentieth century (mainly coal) and then declined. The parallel side-by-side course of the A56, the canal and the railway, was the main factor which led to competition for traffic. Watling Street was a historic straight route running between mosslands, **Fig. 1**. The canal had to follow a contour which by chance was the level of the road, and by running immediately east of the road, the canal company did not have to build so many bridges for minor roads as it would have had to do if the canal had been farther west. At Broadheath the canal cut through the Roman line of Watling Street from Davenport Lane to Highgate and stopped the use of that route[185] for by-passing Altrincham.

Manchester Ship Canal has been in existence since 1894, less than half the time of the Bridgewater. It was built because Manchester manufacturers saw the drift of industry to ports, and being faced with high transport charges from Liverpool, wished to create a port of Manchester. The route of the canal, like the earlier Bridgewater canal does not follow a straight line. This is because it occupies the valley of the Irwell and lower Mersey. In north-east Trafford the canal follows a major meander of the Irwell cut out of solid rock as far as Barton. In this stretch, due to the cutting of the ship canal, Throstle Nest mills were separated from their source of water-power. From Barton the ship canal followed a sweeping course along the Irwell valley. To cope with the fall in level of the previous rivers Irwell and Mersey, locks were built at Mode Wheel, Barton and Irlam. The upper Mersey was prevented from causing downcutting by building a weir at its confluence with the canal near Carrington. At Millbank the canal cuts through solid rock (which had given the head of water to power the mills). Downstream another wide valley opened until restricted again at Warburton. The narrow reaches of Barton and Warburton were bridged.[186] An artificial waterway replaced a natural one and became the geographical and political boundary of north and west Trafford.

Railways

The first railway was the Manchester South Junction and Altrincham Railway completed in 1849, **Fig. 22b**, which passed near the Liverpool Road terminus at Castlefield nearly two decades after that first railway enterprise. With stations on the MSJ&AR close to each other it was a commuter line from the outset. Workers and employers living in Altrincham and Bowdon could avoid the weary drive by private carriage or horse-bus to and from Manchester. The sphere of influence of the latter increased and Altrincham became the main south-western suburb of Manchester. The dates of stations[187] such as Brooklands 1859 (named after Samuel Brooks's estates) and Warwick Road 1931 (sports areas) chronicle later developments.

The MSJ&AR also found the strip of land next to the Bridgewater Canal a flat route where it could compete with the canal trade near the canal wharves. Lord Egerton who owned the canal and adjacent land was also involved in the railway. Commuting to Manchester was aided by the development of horse bus, and, later, petrol-driven bus circular routes to stations. Extension into Cheshire from 1862 assisted the build-up of places such as Hale. Today there is little freight on this line except limestone from Derbyshire via Stockport and Skelton Junction for mid-Cheshire chemical works. After 1923 the Trafford lines, MSJ&AR and CLC continued in joint ownership by the LMS and LNER companies and in 1948 became part of British Rail. Electrification from 1931 did not spread south of Altrincham, and this restriction resulted in the continued use of steam and later diesel trains through into Cheshire. Altrincham became the terminus for the electric Metro tram from 1992. The railway of north Trafford through Urmston in 1873 was also a commuter line, with Trafford Park station, 1904 and Chassen Road, 1934 marking industrial and residential development respectively. The two ex-CLC lines of south Trafford running westwards were mainly long distance passenger and freight lines. The Lymm line was popular for holidaymakers to north Wales until the 1960s when it closed for passengers and was then used by coal trains. The Partington line was used for freight until Irlam steel works closed but continued to supply Carrington power station with coal until that closed in the mid-1990s. Trafford Park had a large system of 56 kilometres (35 miles) operated by its own railway company. Other smaller railways were the line from Altrincham station to Moss Lane gas works and the narrow gauge 'industrial' lines in Davyhulme sewage works and on Carrington Moss, the last concerned with draining, and dumping sewage.

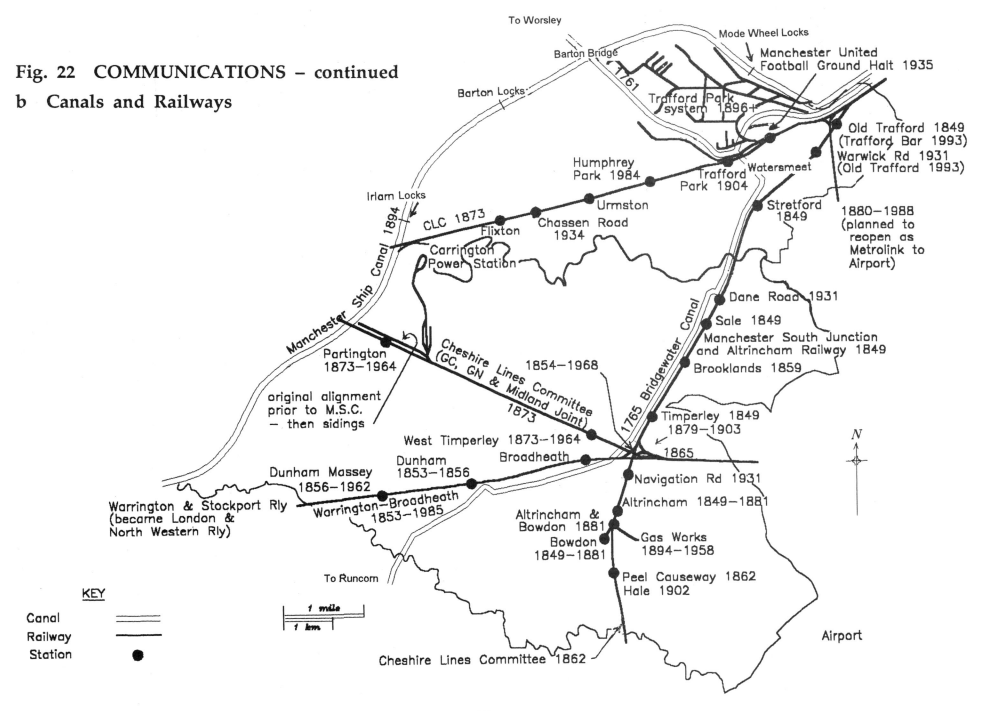

Fig. 22 COMMUNICATIONS – continued

b Canals and Railways

To Worsley

Mode Wheel Locks

Manchester United
Football Ground Halt 1935

Barton Bridge

Barton Locks

Trafford Park
system 1896+

Old Trafford 1849
(Trafford Bar 1993)

Warwick Rd 1931
(Old Trafford 1993)

Humphrey
Park 1984

Trafford
Park 1904

Watersmeet

Stretford
1849

Irlam Locks

CLC 1873

Urmston

1880–1988
(planned to
reopen as
Metrolink to
Airport)

Flixton

Chassen Road
1934

Carrington
Power Station

Dane Road 1931

Sale 1849

Manchester South Junction
and Altrincham Railway 1849

Brooklands 1859

Partington
1873–1964

Cheshire Lines Committee
(GC, GN & Midland Joint)
1873

1854–1968

original alignment
prior to M.S.C.
– then sidings

Timperley 1849
1879–1903

West Timperley 1873–1964

Broadheath

1865

Dunham
1853–1856

Navigation Rd 1931

Warrington & Stockport Rly
(became London &
North Western Rly)

Dunham Massey
1856–1962

Warrington-Broadheath
1853–1985

Altrincham 1849–1881

Altrincham &
Bowdon 1881

Bowdon
1849–1881

Gas Works
1894–1958

Peel Causeway 1862
Hale 1902

To Runcorn

Airport

N

KEY

Canal

Railway

Station

1 mile

1 km

Cheshire Lines Committee 1862

Fig. 23 INDUSTRIAL AREAS

The main development of industry in Trafford was on land obtained from the two great landed families, the Stamfords and the Traffords. A machine-tool and associated industry began in Broadheath in the 1880s, **Fig. 23a**,[188] by, in three cases, foreign engineering firms attracted to a green environment, on land leased from the Earl of Stamford. The site had not long since ceased to be a heath, was cheap, and its industrial premises could not be seen easily from Dunham Hall or Altrincham. Products flowed to the ends of the earth. In pattern it was linear, from east to west, based on the canal and railway, with restricted access from the Manchester road.

In 1896 following the opening of the Manchester Ship Canal, Sir Humphrey de Trafford wished to sell his park for a leisure area but was dissuaded from doing so. The biggest industrial park in Europe, diamond-shaped, was created from his new and old parks and other lands, **Fig. 23b**.[189] To a greater extent than Broadheath, Trafford Park relied on its railway system, and was difficult of road access. Its internal rectangular pattern of roads and railways was American in style reflecting the foreign investment.

Both areas had villages and their own canal, power supplies and railways. Trafford Park even had an aerodrome. The Park was to surpass Broadheath in scale, benefiting from the proximity to Manchester and Salford docks by providing warehousing and ship services. Unevenly, the two areas repeated the mirror-images of north and south Trafford.

The great industrial area of Trafford Park (1,200 acres), and its lesser sister of Broadheath (250 acres) flourished until after World War II. They were particularly busy during the two world wars. Decline started in the 1960s, the reason being, in the case of some of the precision and machine-tool industries of Broadheath, reduced demand and asset-stripping by extraneous take-over companies. Trafford Park's labour force dropped from 75,000 to 24,000[190] but a score of major firms continued. It was reinvigorated by a Development Corporation formed in 1987. The decline of engineering saw a retrenchment and the introduction of retail warehousing, particularly at Broadheath, which was not eligible for urban rescue money nor had a development corporation, though a business centre encouraged activities of all kinds.

A third industrial area was added after World War II at Carrington and Partington. The former had a large power station (completed 1956[191] and closed in 1995) and a huge petro-chemical complex and Partington had a large gas undertaking. **Fig. 23c**[192] shows the rectangular pattern of roads and buildings connected with these complexes. Recent decline in activity at Carrington was countered to some extent by the creation of a business park.

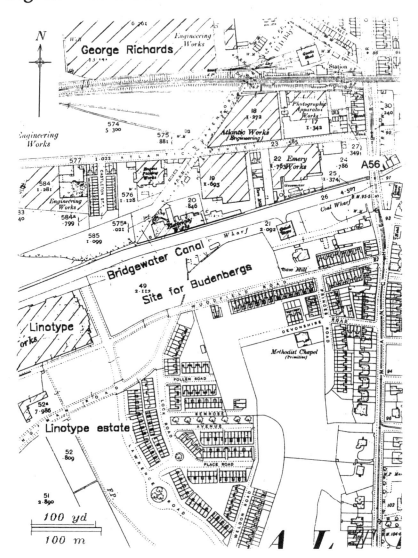

a Broadheath 1910

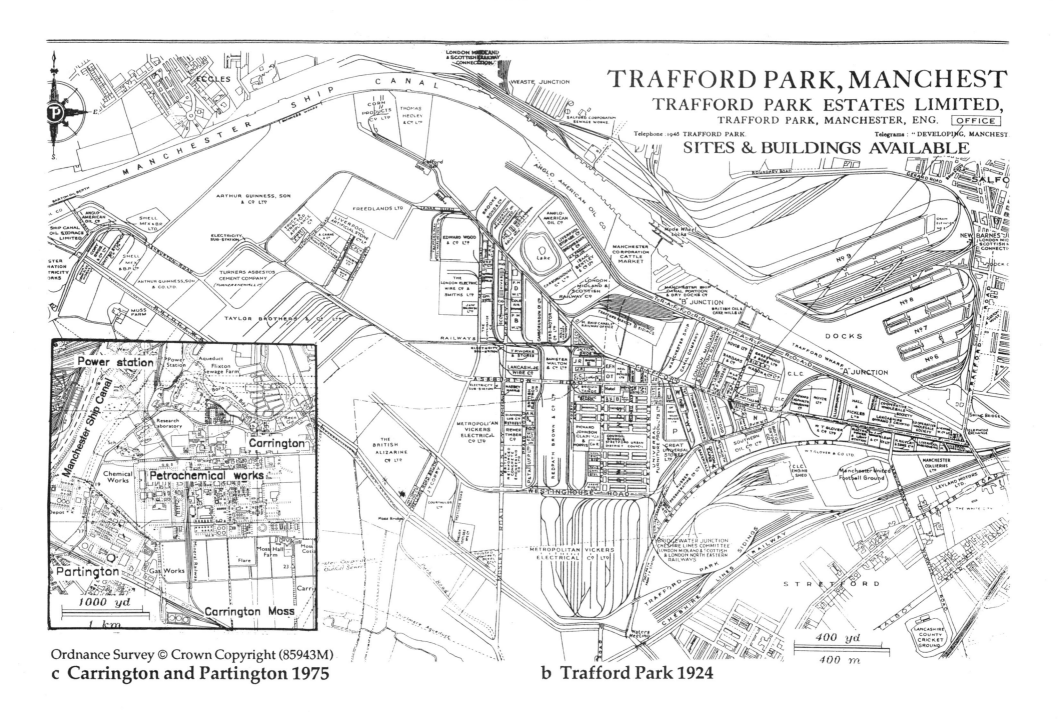

Ordnance Survey © Crown Copyright (85943M)

c Carrington and Partington 1975

b Trafford Park 1924

53

24 LOCAL GOVERNMENT

With the growth of population and the physical size of places the forms of local government and justice through the ancient courts such as halmote, court leet and court baron could not cope. The principle had been for a halmote or court leet to meet once or twice a year to carry out two functions. First, to arrange for local government to be carried out at the behest of the lord of the manor. Second, to apply justice over minor cases of misdemeanour. The court elected a bailiff to run the administration or had the lord's bailiff or other officer imposed, or in the case of Altrincham, a mayor elected each year. In its local government role the court selected unpaid officers nominated from the inhabitants to carry out the offices of constable, surveyor, market looker, swine looker, cattle looker, common looker, dog muzzler, ale taster and others. The last working officer of the Altrincham Court Leet regulated the market until the 1880s. Occasionally the courts had a periodic roll-call serving to check on the number and status of the important inhabitants. A three-weekly court baron using the juries nominated by the main court tried minor misdemeanours. It required certain injustices to be put right and levied fines up to £2 which went into the lord's coffers.

Some court leets ran on through the nineteenth century in even big towns, but it became increasingly difficult for urban districts to cope especially with public health. Through much of the nineteenth century the church vestries, the towns meetings and the overseers of the poor were also involved in administering the affairs of larger places. A government enquiry on municipal corporations in 1834[193] criticised what was happening in the borough of Altrincham and complained that the systems used were incapable of working efficiently. In 1848 under the Public Health Act another government inspector criticised squalor in the town and this led to a Local Board of Health being elected in 1851 to administer the roads, water supply, drainage and sewage and noxious industries. To counter the dangers to public health this new and more efficient system operated at first by the side of the old courts which became more cere-monial than operational as time went on. The elected mayors continued alongside the chairmen of the new U.D. Council until Altrincham became a Municipal Borough in 1937 when the mayoralty was invested in the new borough.[194] The Court Leet was revived in 1977 for ceremonial purposes.

Urban and Rural Sanitary Districts emerged in the last quarter of the nineteenth century with increased powers and constituent civil parishes were created, often coincident with ancient townships. Following the Local Government Act of 1894, Urban and Rural Districts were created, Fig. 24.[195] Some places could have a number of different 'denominations'. For example, Warburton was an ancient township, an ecclesiastical parish and also a civil parish in Bucklow Rural District. Fig. 24 shows that from the late nineteenth century, Flixton and Davyhulme Civil Parishes were in Barton-on-Irwell Rural District and Partington, Warburton, Dunham Massey, Carrington, Timperley in Bucklow Rural District. Several Urban Districts were created in or shortly after 1894: Stretford, Urmston, Ashton-on-Mersey, Sale, Altrincham, Bowdon and Hale. There was a power struggle in the south where Altrincham tried for decades to absorb Bowdon and Hale and failed. Powerful Urban Districts wished to extend their boundaries to provide more land to house their growing populations. Stretford had acquired part of Davyhulme and was subsequently declared the first Municipal Borough in 1933. Altrincham absorbed parts of Dunham Massey and Carrington in the 1920s and 1930s and eventually all Timperley in 1936 and so was large enough to be declared a Municipal Borough in 1937. By its acquisition of Timperley it increased its size of population from 22000 to 36000. The general similarity between Figs. 24 and 14 is striking. The pattern of administrative districts up to 1974 was, for many parts of Trafford, the same as it had been for a thousand years or more, and though status changed, the old boundaries were still in use.

Fig. 24 RECENT ADMINISTRATIVE AREAS TO 1974

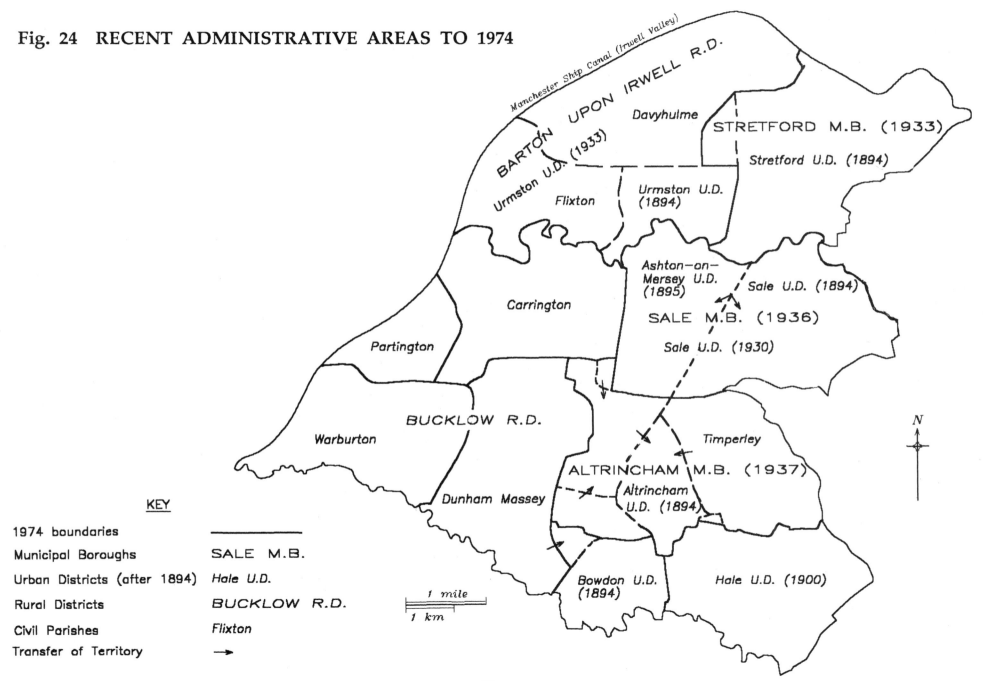

Manchester Ship Canal (Irwell Valley)

BARTON UPON IRWELL R.D.

Davyhulme

STRETFORD M.B. (1933)

Urmston U.D. (1933)

Stretford U.D. (1894)

Flixton

Urmston U.D. (1894)

Ashton-on-Mersey U.D. (1895)

Sale U.D. (1894)

SALE M.B. (1936)

Carrington

Sale U.D. (1930)

Partington

BUCKLOW R.D.

Warburton

Timperley

ALTRINCHAM M.B. (1937)

Dunham Massey

Altrincham U.D. (1894)

N

KEY

1974 boundaries	———
Municipal Boroughs	SALE M.B.
Urban Districts (after 1894)	Hale U.D.
Rural Districts	BUCKLOW R.D.
Civil Parishes	Flixton
Transfer of Territory	→

Bowdon U.D. (1894)

Hale U.D. (1900)

1 mile

1 km

25 THE EARLY TWENTIES

Fig. 25[196] shows that urbanisation and industrialisation had made some progress towards the modern position. Old Trafford was contiguous with Manchester in one direction and almost attached to Gorse Hill and Stretford on the other but Flixton and Urmston were not yet joined. In the south, Altrincham, Hale and Bowdon had become a mini-conurbation but the smaller neighbours of Altrincham had preserved their political independence. The main spread of inter-war private and council building was yet to come. A clear impression of the social values of the period is given by emphasis through the blocking or heavy shading of industry, infrastructure and dense populations in 'black' on the map. This is especially marked in Trafford Park, Broadheath, and at Davyhulme sewage works. Not only roads and main railways are shown but also light railways (tramways). Wharves, locks, cemeteries and golf facilities were also indicated, but not power lines, for defence reasons.

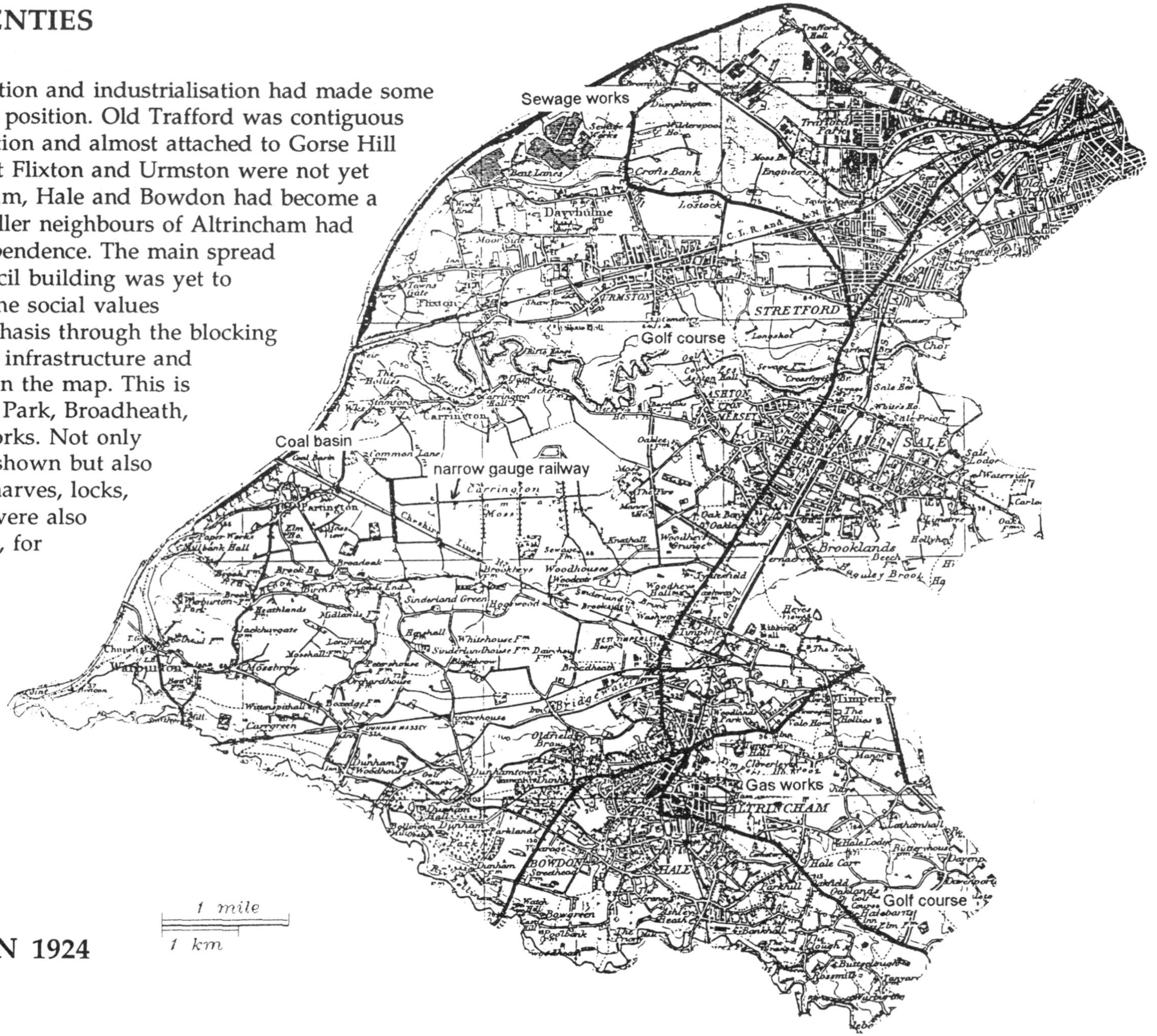

Fig. 25   TRAFFORD IN 1924

26 AT THE END OF WORLD WAR II

The area immediately after World War II and well before it received borough status in 1974 is shown in **Fig. 26**.[197] The Manchester Ship Canal and the Mersey formed the administrative boundary between Lancashire and Cheshire. The emphasis was on industry and dense housing (shown black). Housing, when compared with the previous map, can be seen to be intensifying along the eastern corridor of communications and into north-western Trafford. There were two mini-conurbations, one in north Trafford where it was possible to travel from Flixton to Old Trafford without passing through open space, and one from Sale through Brooklands, Timperley and Altrincham to Bowdon where the only differentiating features between places were the road signs announcing them. Most of the great inter-war estates, private and council had been built such as Woodheys, Timperley, Oldfield Brow, Stretford, Urmston and Flixton, but the following areas were not yet built: north Davyhulme, Manor Avenue district in Sale, Partington, Bowdon Vale and Hale Barns. The Carrington power station and chemicals complex and Partington gas plants had still to appear and there were no motorways.

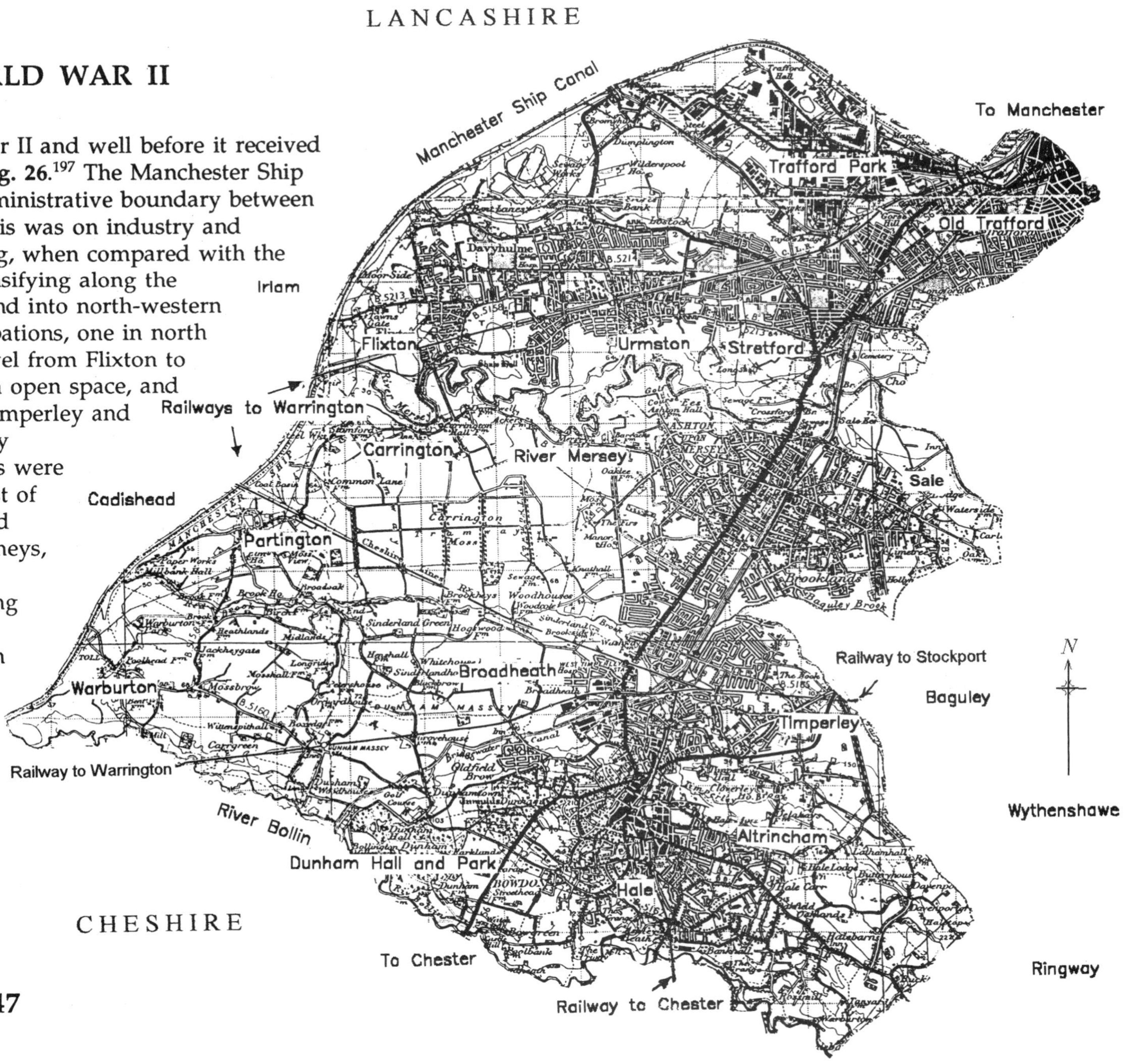

Fig. 26 TRAFFORD IN 1947

27 TRAFFORD IN 1951

By 1951[198] the population in total was 202,232 having more than doubled since 1901. The populations of both north and south Trafford were almost equal. Four places, two on each side of the Mersey were very large. These were Stretford, the largest (61,874) and Urmston (39,237) in the north; Sale (43,168) and Altrincham (39,787) in the south.

There were two modest sized Urban Districts, Hale (12,152) and Bowdon (3,524), vulnerable to take-over, and a number of small civil parishes in Bucklow Rural District with tiny populations between 376 and 957. The northern c.p.s of the former Barton-on-Irwell R.D. had been incorporated in Urmston U.D. in 1933.

Details of the distribution of towns and occupations at this time can be seen in **Fig. 27**. Stretford Municipal Borough, Urmston U.D. and Altrincham M.B. had the greatest proportion of their populations in manufacturing whereas Sale M.B. (which had absorbed Ashton-on-Mersey U.D. in 1930), Hale and Bowdon U.D.s showed a greater percentage in services.

Agriculture was still present to a small extent in the eastern authorities of Hale, Bowdon and Sale for which statistics were available but was minimal in the other larger places. This activity would have been more important in the smaller western places but figures were not available in the census for rural civil parishes in R.D.s.

Though a familiar part of the modern scene, Carrington and Partington had little industry at this date; the great chemical works and gasworks were to yet to come, also the power station which was to dominate the skyline but to have only a short life.

The four census-derived maps from 1801 to 1951 have shown to a common scale the immense population explosion during Trafford's exposure to the industrial, communications and commercial revolution when emphasis shifted from agriculture to manufacturing, commerce and services. The decline of agriculture has been very great with farmland output changing from arable to milk products and vegetables because of different demands as time has passed. Farming practices were disrupted due to invasion by roads and housing leading to neglected land, and its use for market gardening, horses and tips. Unfortunately over the period 1801-1951 the picture is not certain because government figures grouped statistics under headings which changed from one census to another. This has not made it possible to get a truly comparable sequence.

Fig. 27 POPULATION AND OCCUPATIONS 1951

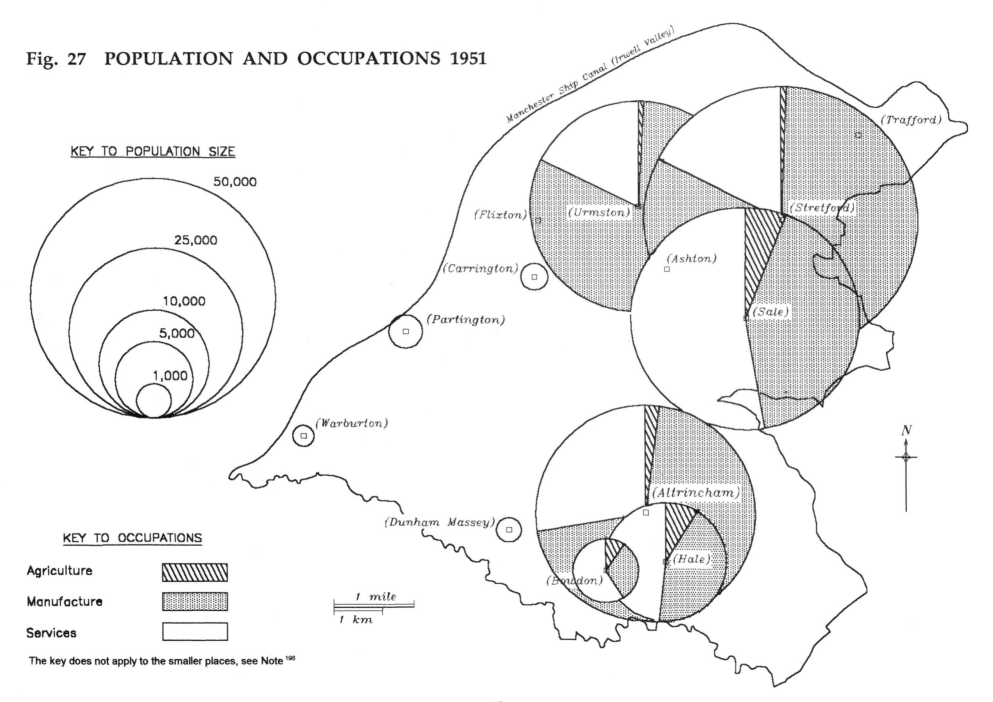

KEY TO POPULATION SIZE

50,000
25,000
10,000
5,000
1,000

KEY TO OCCUPATIONS

Agriculture

Manufacture

Services

The key does not apply to the smaller places, see Note [198]

Manchester Ship Canal (Irwell Valley)

(Trafford)

(Flixton) *(Urmston)* *(Stretford)*

(Carrington) *(Ashton)*

(Partington) *(Sale)*

(Warburton)

(Altrincham)

(Dunham Massey) *(Hale)*

(Bowdon)

1 mile

1 km

N

59

Changes in planning styles

The examples from Trafford which follow do not include modern shopping malls or town redevelopment schemes. The types are mainly based on changes in planning ideas and policies for residential areas.

1. Regimented terrace housing

The building of terraces was seen as an efficient and attractive way to house the sudden increase of population generated by industrialisation. Gorse Hill (a) was a completely planned urban village[199] built on a 'greenfield' site about 1900 mainly for workers commuting to Manchester and Trafford Park. It had a church, shops, school and park. It was fairly near the railway but profited later from the presence of trams and buses. This is in contrast to terraces appended to and dependent upon the infrastructure of existing population centres, for example, at Stretford (b)[200] where rectangular blocks of streets were added to an existing old town centre. This development was also dependent on public transport facilities. Central Trafford Park (c)[201] attracted a number of foreign firms and shows a rectangular American style planning of buildings, and a village of terraced houses which fitted in with early twentieth century planning. Note the American style street names. The plan was also affected by the size of radii of curves necessary for the railways which ran along the roads.

2. The planners' reaction to regimentation 1900-14

The pattern of roads on the Linotype estate of 1907, **Fig. 23a**, introduced gentle geometric curves. Roads were named after directors. Planners were influenced by the idea of 'garden suburbs' with rustic-type cottages and leafy rural avenues.

3. The housing problem of the inter-war years

Planners in the 1920s were faced with the problem of a rising demand for housing after soldiers returned home after World War I. The Oldfield Brow council estate of 407 houses (d)[202] was begun in the 1920s with a pattern of formal circles and closes typical of the times. Davyhulme (e)[203] was designed in the same period for private owners; its plan was a pure geometrical exercise.

4. The control of landlords on style and layout

In upper Altrincham (f)[204] mansions were built at a low density at fairly regular distances apart to designs approved by Lord Stamford. In Sale (g)[205] there was more regularity to the pattern of the large houses, stylishly arranged round the Sale United Reform Church in Montague Road.

5. Post World War II estates in spacious settings

In more recent times where available land was not so constrained there was less geometrical regimentation and a more relaxed relationship between planning and the land available. At Hale Barns (h)[206] private detached and semi-detached houses in car commuter-land can be seen along wide roads which follow gentle curves. There is a school but no nearby shops; these can be reached by car.

6. Post World War II housing in cramped areas

Faced with replacement of bombed and worn-out properties in densely-peopled areas, planners were obliged to house rapidly large numbers of people in small areas. Old Trafford (i)[207] shows the pattern of high rise flats. The large open spaces between the towers were necessary because the planners had to think in three dimensions in order to make necessary space and light available as required by planning regulations; while there are some 'closes', other spaces have been upgraded to 'courts'. The rectangularity of the plan of the flats had to be fitted within the ancient naturally curved boundary along the Cornbrook between Trafford and Manchester. The shape of Loreto College (just over the Manchester side of the boundary) also shows the effect of the curved boundary. There was also a return to terrace housing believed to be desired by the local people.

Fig. 28   CHANGES IN PLANNING STYLES

North is at the top of the map unless otherwise indicated. Scales vary. Names have been added.

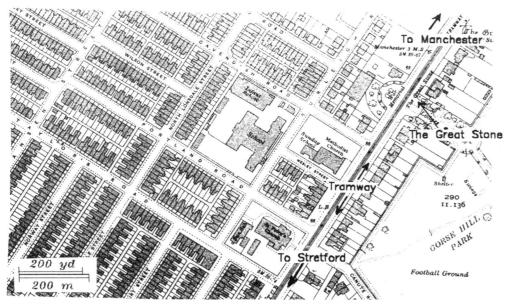

a Gorse Hill 1931 A planned urban village with church, shops, school and park built around 1900, after Trafford Park. Workers commuted by tram, bus or bike. The Great Stone is thought to be part of a Saxon cross, perhaps from near St Matthew's.

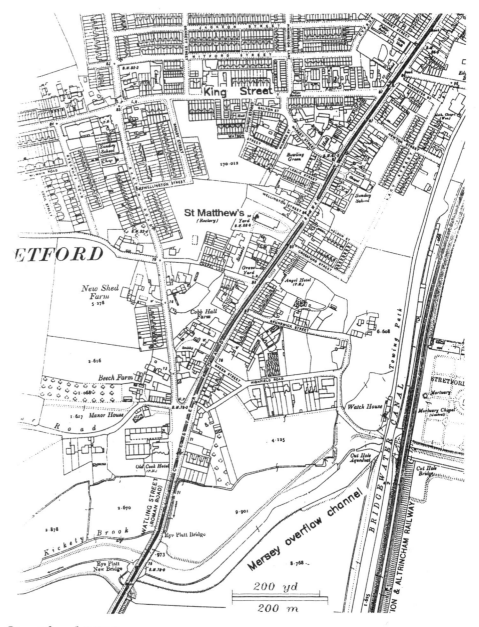

b Stretford 1910 Blocks of terraces were clearly separate from the old street village around St Matthew's. Many people worked in Manchester or Trafford Park. The road, rail and canal head south towards the Mersey.

Fig. 28 CHANGES IN PLANNING STYLES

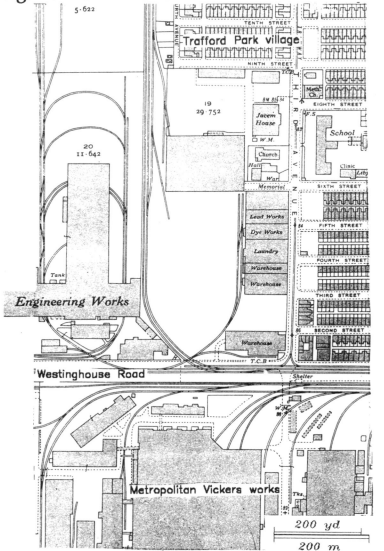

c Central Trafford Park 1937 The American influence can be seen in planning and street names. The giant electrical engineers (later AEI and GEC Alsthom) and the village have been demolished.

d Oldfield Brow 1938 Built in a geometrical design typical of the period mainly to house workers from Broadheath. More flats were built after the war.

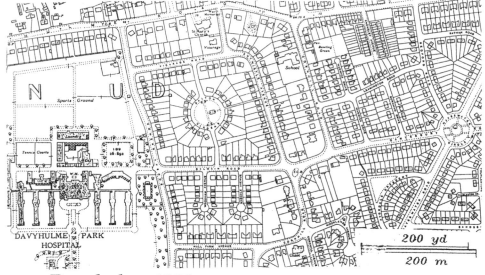

e Davyhulme 1937 The inter-war housing pattern was straight off the drawing board; even the hospital was aligned due north and south.

Fig. 28 CHANGES IN PLANNING STYLES – continued

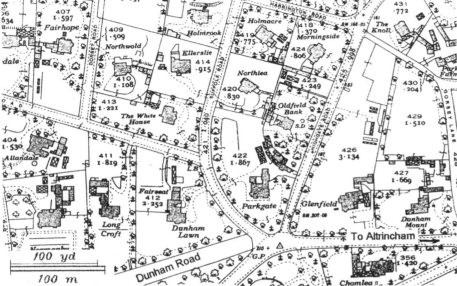

f Upper Altrincham 1910 The mansions were built at low density per acre according to the rules laid down by Lord Stamford

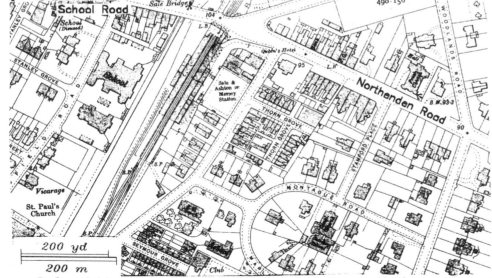

g Sale 1910 Villas were laid out in a planned fashion and had easy access to the station.

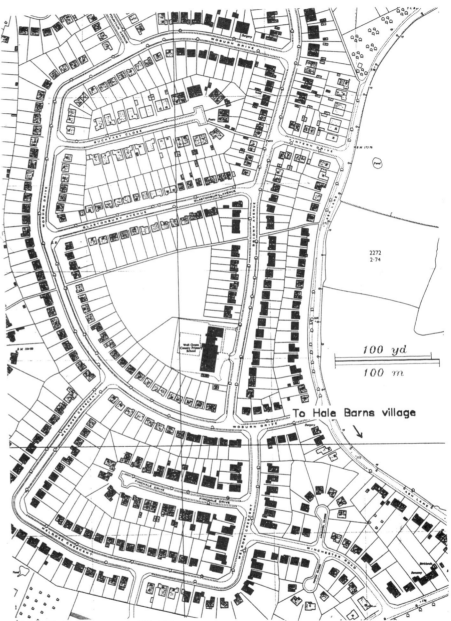

h Hale Barns 1967 Detached and semi-detached in car commuterland. The geometry is not so regular as at Davyhulme.

63

Fig. 28 CHANGES IN PLANNING STYLES – continued

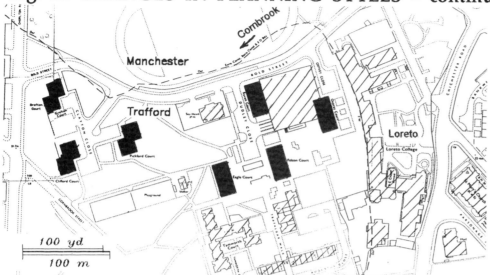

i Old Trafford 1980 The pattern of high rise flats (shown black). The overall plan had to be fitted into the curved Trafford boundary of the Cornbrook which had even affected the shape of buildings such as Loreto College.

Sports Areas

A remarkable leisure pattern: Trafford's major sports grounds
Old Trafford (j)[208] shows a striking three-point pattern made by the location of three famous sports areas for football, cricket and dog-racing. The White City dog track (now a retail park) lay on the site of the Royal Botanical Gardens of late Victorian times. These facilities might have been linked with a late nineteenth century project to make the whole of Trafford Park a leisure area rather than an industrial zone (Sir Humphrey de Trafford wished for this; the author's mother remembered boating on the park's lake, now in Trafford Ecology Park). However, Trafford Park became industrialised and the plan which would probably have given Trafford perhaps the largest leisure complex of its day did not materialise.

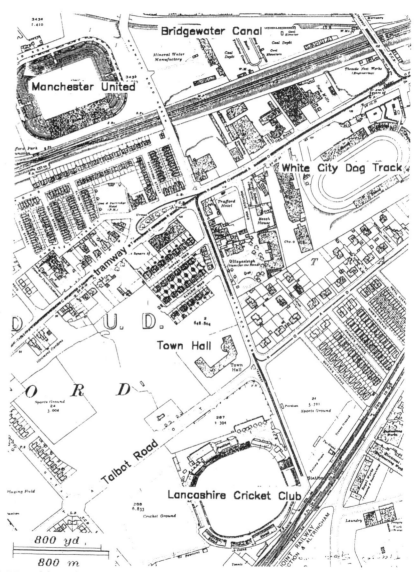

j Old Trafford sports areas 1931 It is curious how this area attracted a group of major regional leisure facilities.

Types of Growth

Four examples

i. At Flixton (k)[209] the medieval core of the village was round St Michael's. There was no hall. Flixton House is eighteenth century. After the railway was built in 1873, commuting began and terraces were built along roads called Albert Avenue and Victoria Avenue. After World War I property was built over the railway in Devon Road and Western Road. Flixton could not expand south because of the Mersey valley, liable to flood, nor to the west because of school grounds, nor to the east because of golf courses; it could only spread northwards to the Davyhulme boundary and northwestwards along the Ship Canal banks.

ii. The old centre of Urmston (l)[210] lay just east of the station and the hall to the south. The station area became the focus and Victorian property was built round it and as far, in the map extract shown, as the north-south Flixton boundary so that the youngest property is in general furthest from the old centre. Like Flixton it could not spread south because of the Mersey. To the north it was blocked by the Davyhulme hospital and estates and to the east lay the Stretford boundary. It absorbed Flixton and Davyhulme in 1933 to become a U.D.

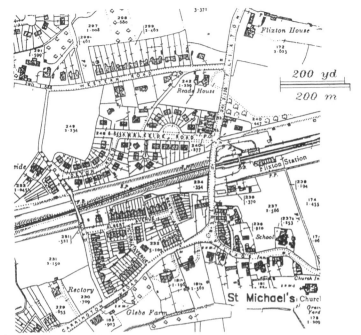

k Flixton 1928 The original settlement was a T-junction village round St Michael's. After 1873 terraces filled the gap to the station. Later, twentieth century property leap-frogged over the line northwards.

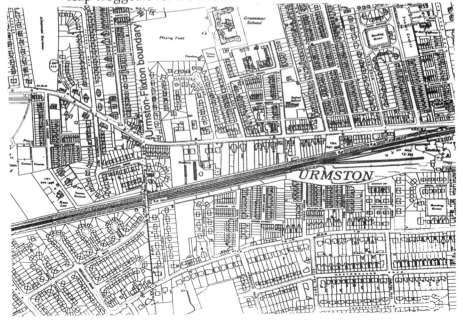

l Urmston 1937 Urmston station and village lie to the east (right). After the railway came in 1873 building spread westwards and also away from the railway. A boundary line to the west separates Urmston and Flixton and a marked change of building pattern can be seen on either side of this line. Urmston incorporated Flixton in 1933 and was then able to spread west into it. At one time Stretford wished to join with Urmston to avoid a take-over by Manchester but this never took place.

iii. In a different fashion, present Hale, on the Altrincham map (m) grew not from an old centre but from a railway station built where the road from Altrincham to Bowdon crossed Broomfield Lane and the Ashley Road in 1862. The economic centre moved here from Hale Barns and building spreading from 'new' Hale eventually engulfed the older village of Hale Barns.

iv. Altrincham (m)[211] is worth examining in some detail because it was an ancient borough. The growth by 1910 had been complex due to constraints of land:

1. The old core of Market Place and George Street was pre-railway in date. Railway Street and Stamford New Road were completed around the turn of this century.

2. The town was able to extend north as far as Broadheath in small developments which occurred in the 1920s and 30s.

3. The town could not easily extend to the north-east in early times because the land was in Timperley (Old Hall Farm) and building stopped at Timperley Brook; the land was also ill-drained. Eastwards towards Hale Barns there was Hale Moss, not finally reclaimed until the 1880s, a claypit, gas-works and brickworks. Some building had been carried out up to the boundary with Hale U.D., where at Urban Road the first council estate was begun by 1908. Building did not take place beyond Queens Road until the 1920s, shown by 'empty' blocks on the map – planned sites for buildings.

4. Altrincham had extended north-west and south-west into the town field (where the burgesses formerly had their plots) when the power of the Court Leet waned after the establishment of a Local Board in 1851.

5. From mid-nineteenth century building had extended further west into Dunham Massey township encouraged by Lord Stamford who owned the land. Mansions filled some of the area (f). This tract was in reality an extension of the built-up area of Altrincham and was eventually incorporated into the town in the 1920s and part provided a site for the Oldfield Brow estate.

6. To the south-west Bowdon township (U.D. 1894) was already filled with villas and larger properties, many established from the mid-nineteenth century and this blocked major development in that direction.

7. South of Altrincham centre strips of the old town field were early sold off by individual owners for terraced cottage property round New Street from 1800. Newtown was a late nineteenth century terraced development near Bowdon Station (Lloyd Street). Many servants who worked in the bigger houses lived here.

8. The land to the south-east lay in Hale township (U.D. 1901) where there had been terrace building in the last quarter of the nineteenth century.

By 1910 western Hale and northern Bowdon were contiguous with Altrincham. Timperley was absorbed in 1936 and its urbanisation proceeded apace, with Altrincham extending rapidly north-east. Growth to the east itself was still inhibited by the golf course, brickworks, gasworks and other industrial units such as a motorcycle factory and there were also many market gardens. Today virtually the whole of the map area is built up apart from the south Timperley tract and an area north-west of the Bridgewater Canal.

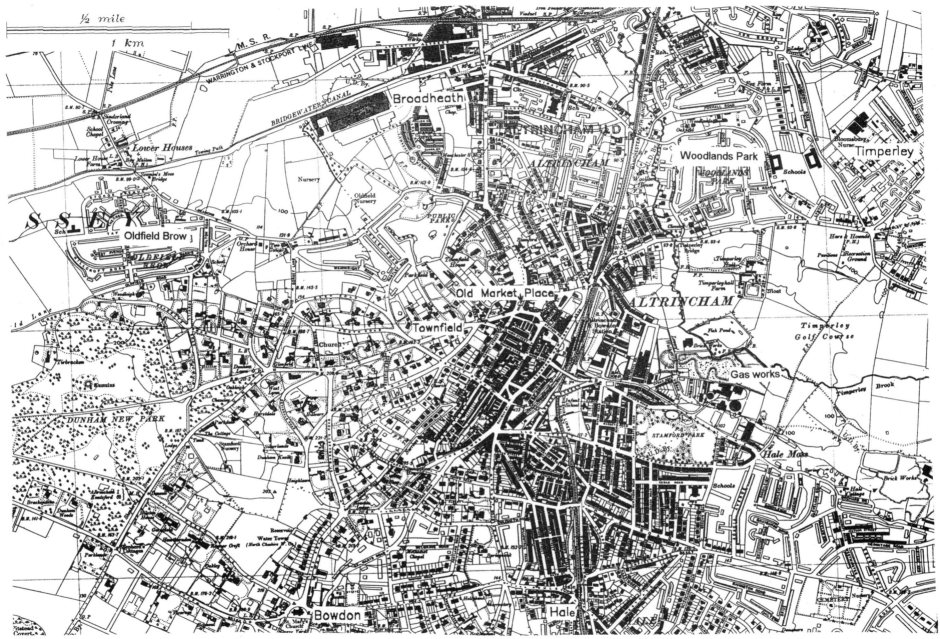

m Altrincham and Hale 1910   With additions to 1938. Buildings erected before 1910 are shaded, those built after 1910 but not surveyed fully for this 1938 edition are included in 'empty' blocks such as in Woodlands Park (to the north-east) and Oldfield Brow (to the north-west).

29 RECENT TIMES

If **Fig. 29**[212] reflects changes in social thinking, it shows the rising importance of road transport, leisure, power and other infrastructure. It does not show the turbulent post-World War II political history which led to the creation of the boundary of Trafford in 1974 used in this atlas. Trafford possessed three Municipal Boroughs but Manchester City and some other powerful authorities in Greater Manchester such as Bury and Stockport had County Borough status and the problem arose as to how disparate authorities could co-operate. Ideas were floated for the creation of super-authorities to co-ordinate regional planning and other systems. In one of these proposals Cheshire was to disappear completely. It was perhaps no coincidence that *The Historical Atlas of Cheshire* (see Note 1) published in the late 1950s reflected the commitment of Cheshire people to retain their county.

A major feature of post-war life was the expansion of public transport and in order to regulate this, local transport departments were grouped into the South East Lancashire and North East Cheshire authority (SELNEC) also used for strategic planning. In 1974 SELNEC's powers were subsumed by a new Greater Manchester County, which still exists though its Council was abolished in 1986.

In 1966-67 the Local Government Commission under Lord Redcliffe-Maud recommended the creation of new regions with Metropolitan Borough status. Planners wanted to link places where commuters lived with their places of work. One district was proposed to extend from Sale to Winsford. However, Derek Senior, one of the planners, put in a 300 page Note of Dissent, recommending a region with a population of 300,000 including much of present Trafford, Eccles and part of south Manchester. Senior's views were largely accepted and after some trimming the boundaries of Trafford Metropolitan Borough were drawn up and Trafford began life in 1974.

Population in Trafford rose to 212,731 in 1991 and the processes of urbanisation and industrialisation had culminated by 1995 in two large and one smaller mini-conurbations, **Fig. 29**. One large zone extended from Davyhulme to Old Trafford, the other from Sale and Ashton to Hale. The third zone was the new industrial and power complex of Partington and Carrington, Partington also being a major residential area. North Trafford had long been connected to Manchester; by this date Sale and Timperley had also become contiguous with the metropolis. The west of Trafford though still mainly a farming area had been invaded by residences, sewage works, electricity pylons, a crematorium and golf courses. Nineteenth century maps showed an explosion in the number of churches, the twentieth showed an explosion in the number of large areas occupied by schools.

On **Figs. 25** (1924) and **26** (1947) the industrial and urban districts had been strongly identified in black. In **Fig. 29**, the shift of social values is seen in the fact that they were both shaded pale brown in the original map (not clear on the black and white map printed here, **Fig. 29**). The industrial areas had passed their peak of development and do not show as many works as on maps of earlier decades. The emphasis had changed to clarity of the road pattern, including the motorways reflecting the car age. The Carrington spur can be seen, crossing an important bridge over the Mersey. In the Middle Ages Altrincham market had a catchment area of radius three miles. With the car and bus this catchment had increased from 7 miles into Cheshire in 1974 to 15 miles by 1985.[213] The development of personal and public transport was to change the historic dependence of people on the local place as the only source of goods. Hence the need for clear roads on the map.

Some of the added labels show features[214] instituted recently under Trafford M.B. since 1974: the new Centenary Bridge across Manchester Ship Canal from Eccles built in 1994, a hundred years after the opening of the canal, and new roadworks at Old Trafford, both to improve entry into Trafford Park. Conservation areas, business parks and areas affected by local plans are too small to show. Sale Water Park and some footpaths are shown and also the dismantled western railway which will be part of the Trans-Pennine footpath. Additionally the large marshalling yard in Trafford Park is now a huge Euroterminal. The remnant of Trafford Park's Victorian ornamental lake is an educational Ecology Park. There is unfortunately little indication of the vast improvements in Trafford Park started by the Development Corporation or of other environmental improvement.

Fig. 29 TRAFFORD IN 1995

The airport and M56 are shown because of their importance to Trafford, though the airport is not in the borough and only a short stretch of the M56 touches the boundary.

Ordnance Survey © Crown Copyright (85943M)

1 mile

1 km

30 TRAFFORD IN THE FUTURE

Fig. 30 is a sketch map[215] derived from larger more detailed maps in the Unitary Development Plan, a ten-year plan for the borough from 1995. The sketch map does not show details of commercial zones, sports grounds, parks and leisure centres. A major development is The Trafford Centre out-of-town retail centre at Dumplington. Places such as Altrincham and Gorse Hill will have individual local plans. The plan stabilises the development of land-use over the last century as residential across the northern and down the eastern half of the borough with three major industrial sites, Trafford Park, Carrington-Partington and Broadheath. Trafford Park in particular is destined for great investment and improvement. There will be probably a gradual change to accommodate smaller enterprises especially of a service nature in business parks. No vast new housing areas are envisaged. Most of the western side is protected by Green Belt policy and will be reserved for agricultural and other open space uses. Leisure use will be made of some former railway routes, for example, to Partington and Lymm. The Mersey valley, an open space over the centuries between north and south, is becoming a major leisure zone. The former avenue of trade, Manchester Ship Canal, is not likely to be used as such on a large scale above Warrington and its upper reaches may be used for leisure purposes only.

The map shows there has been a revolution in thinking about the central places, however small, with which people were once associated. In historic times Trafford places had interrelations amongst themselves, p.12, and also connections with places outside the area, as described on p.14 but these were really the concern of the lords and higher institutions, such as religious bodies. The connections for ordinary people were with the place which had functions central to their needs, the ancient villages and towns where they lived, shown on many maps in this atlas. Over the last decades and as envisaged for the future, many people now not only live some distance from these older centres but use more than one centre for particular functions and to supply particular needs such as shopping and education. Lives are no longer based on one place, or even on two, such as the home and the workplace, nor is the nearest centre to home necessarily the one most visited.

For example, the pattern of future retail centres shows a new set of ideas about the location of important sites with 'pull' for people. A number of ancient places which have previously been mentioned in this atlas as important in earlier contexts are no longer seen as future centres except for social and a few immediate retail needs. These are Flixton, Davyhulme, Old Trafford, Carrington, Partington, Ashton-on-Mersey, Warburton, Dunham Woodhouses, Dunham Town, Bowdon and Hale Barns. In contrast, places which are now seen in the UDP as having important functions for the future are The Trafford Centre, Urmston, Stretford, Sale, Sale Moor, Broadheath, Timperley, Altrincham and (modern) Hale village. Curiously, about the same number as in historic times but differently distributed, and beginning to show the importance of motorway access. Specialised attractions lie not only in individual retail units in the borough but outside at places such as Manchester, Baguley, Irlam, Cheadle and Handforth.

The chief factors to influence the economic future of Trafford will be i. the effect of The Trafford Centre and out-of-Trafford retail centres on the smaller internal Trafford units, ii. the prosperity or decline of industry and commerce in the borough, iii. the increase or decrease of the importance of retail, business, education (especially higher education) and leisure facilities in Manchester and Salford, and iv. the future of Manchester Airport. The pattern of several of these powerful influences already forms a ring round Trafford. Trafford was extremely powerful in the past, in medieval times because of its military barons, in later centuries because of its great landed gentry and until the 1970s because of its huge industry and commerce. In future it will need to increase its internal strength to withstand outside pressures. The people of Trafford have been connected with outside bodies from ancient times, often from a dominant position, as this atlas has shown, but the problem today is to resist economic and other pressures from outside or use them for Trafford's own well-being or perhaps develop some regional prominence in a particular field.

Fig. 30 TRAFFORD IN THE FUTURE

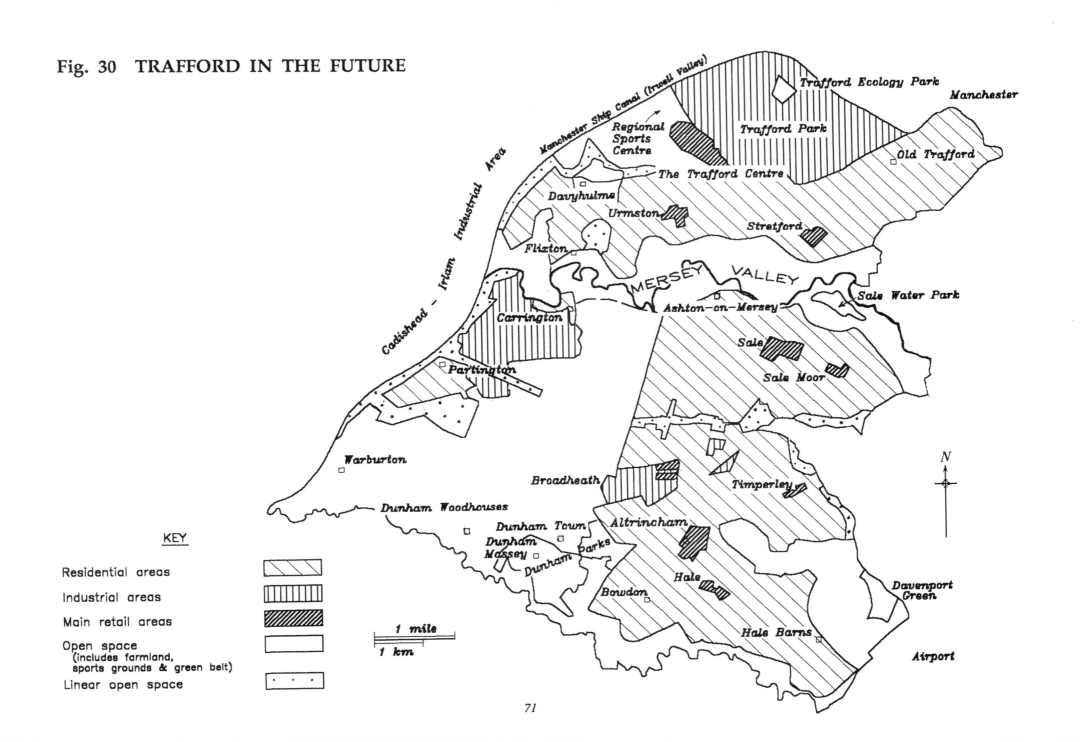

KEY

Residential areas

Industrial areas

Main retail areas

Open space
(includes farmland,
sports grounds & green belt)

Linear open space

1 mile

1 km

31 CONCLUSIONS

Maps are very useful in many ways as planners, military men and walkers can testify. As has been shown in this atlas they can be very informative though they cannot tell the whole history of an area. In particular the personal element is missing, for example, the decision-making involved in settling and developing the land. But the distributions and patterns shown on the maps have been useful in identifying areas of change from one period to another. The maps shown, apart from one or two Jacobean or later maps which have artistic merit but are not very accurate, have been as objective as possible in portraying the development of Trafford to the present. There have been examples, however, where statistics, when mapped, have given the wrong impression, even Government statistics, though no doubt cynics will not be surprised!

One of the interesting features which has emerged from the maps is that in early times there were very significant differences between people and places on either side of the Mersey valley due to its power as a barrier to communications, affecting settlement history and cultural differences. There has been a mirror-like reflection of the two halves of Trafford in historic time, each having in recent centuries an important hall, estate and controlling family, its own industrial zone, each a Municipal Borough (two in the case of south Trafford) and each having different shire loyalties, the north to Lancashire and the south to Cheshire. These earlier differences between north and south might have been thought to have been consigned to oblivion by the creation of Trafford Borough but history is a long time going away. The old areal units still exist in people's minds and in their mental maps of the area. Many places now in Trafford were to a large or small extent self-governing from medieval times until only a generation ago. The time from 1974 is only a moment in Trafford's history and people's memories. Even though many places are now joined by continuous building with only a sign to say where one place begins and another ends, people still associate themselves with the old centres and even past counties.

Though an administrative unit, Trafford is not an historical, urban or social entity and lacks one major centre in contrast to some of the other 1974 boroughs round Greater Manchester. It seems the planners who designed the borough had little sense of the geography of the area. If a new borough centre had been built in the Mersey valley in the middle of Trafford after 1974 it might have created a clear geographical focus. After all, a medieval baron was able to build a new borough in AD1290.

However, the opportunity now arises through the Unitary Development Plan leisure proposals to make the Mersey valley a unifying feature of a new Trafford, uniting north and south rather than being a barrier as it has been in the past.

For the future the major strengths of Trafford are planned to lie in the huge investment in the industrial and commercial redevelopment of Trafford Park, the further development of communications, leisure provision and The Trafford Centre. However, a significant future for the other places in Trafford must not be forgotten. Perhaps different specialisations for different places could be developed just as happened in the great baronies and estates of medieval times outlined earlier in this atlas, in which each place not only had an individuality but also played a complementary role in the prosperity of the whole.

The old local centres now co-exist in one authority. Before 1974 for some administrative practices there was only a distant overview of the Trafford area from Preston or Chester. Since that date Trafford has been one administrative unit, as the previous map shows, and the fact that major decision-making is based locally must be an advantage. Finally, this atlas has shown that there is a wealth of fascinating history in Trafford which could be developed into a tourism policy to which almost every place could make a contribution.

NOTES AND REFERENCES

Abbreviations

Greater Manchester Archaeological Unit	GMAU
Greater Manchester Archaeological Contracts Section	GMAC
University of Manchester Archaeological Unit	UMAU
Trafford Sites and Monuments Record Update Computer Printout	SMR
Trafford Sites and Monuments Record Report	SMR Report
Manchester University Department of Geography	MUDG
John Rylands Library, Deansgate, University of Manchester	Rylands
South Trafford Archaeological Group	STAG
Trafford Local Studies Centre	TLSC
Trafford Metropolitan Borough Council	Trafford MBC
Ordnance Survey	O.S.
Victoria County History series	VCH

INTRODUCTION

1. Sylvester, D. and Nulty, G., *The Historical Atlas of Cheshire*.
2. UMAU, GMAU; GMAC: *The Archaeology of Trafford* – in preparation.

1 THE LANDSCAPE

3. **Fig. 1** and many maps in this atlas (printed with the permission of the Ordnance Survey) use the modern boundary of Trafford Metropolitan Borough for an outline. The Manchester Ship Canal is the modern western boundary and it may seem strange to use this where for centuries the boundary was the rivers Irwell and lower Mersey but this has been done because it is the present reality, and for consistency. **Fig. 1** and other distributions were originally plotted at a scale of 1:50000, then reduced to about 1:70000 to fit the page. The contour has been selected to show the junction of lowland and upland. The names of some places are shown in italics to assist locating features. These points are arbitrary. In maps of periods before 1901 Hale Barns is shown but not modern Hale because the former is believed to have been more important in early times. Dunham Massey Hall site was also important in previous centuries. On the other hand, the Old Trafford site shows the site of the present town hall and not that of the ancient Old Trafford Hall. Small brooks such as the Cornbrook and Ousel Brook are not shown; part of the former is the modern boundary of north-east Trafford. The line of Watling Street is shown on many maps under that name because of its importance in early communications but its parts are now variously called Chester Road, Washway Road, Cross Street, Manchester Road and Dunham Road.
4. Crofton, H.T., *A History of the Ancient Chapel of Stretford, Part I*, Chetham Society, p.30.
5. The distribution of mosses is from Hall, D., Wells, C.E. and Huckerby, E., *The Wetlands of Greater Manchester*; also from the 'Drift' maps of the Geological Survey, Yates's map of Lancashire 1786 and Burdett's map of Cheshire, 1777. The Geological Survey maps record the extent of peat at the survey of 1923-25 by which time it was not as extensive as in former periods. Carrington Moss in mid-nineteenth century was about 3 by 2 kilometres in size and 4 metres deep.

2 GEOLOGY, CLIMATE AND VEGETATION

6. Edwards, W. and Trotter F.M., *British Regional Geology, Pennines and Adjacent Areas*; Hull, E., *The Geology of the Country Round Altrincham*, Geological Survey, 1861.
7. **Fig. 2** compiled from Geological Survey 1:63,360 Manchester and Stockport 'Drift' sheets reduced in scale to about 1:70000.
8. West, R.G., *Pleistocene Geology and Biology*, pp.58, 59 and 369.
9. Darby, H.C., *An Historical Geography of England to 1700*, p.96.
10. West, R.G., *op. cit.*, p.212. Also see Nevell, M., *Tameside 1066-1700*, p.48, for details from the medieval period.

3 PREHISTORIC AND ROMAN TIMES

11. Distributions plotted in **Fig. 3** have been almost wholly based on GMAU Trafford Sites and Monuments Record Update Computer Printout (SMR), 1995. Watling Street (part A56), the A538 and more recent finds have been added. It is assumed Watling Street did not go through central Altrincham. The details of its course are subject to much discussion. It may be too straight as drawn; its line is shown diverted through Altrincham on maps in the atlas representing medieval and later periods. In the text the term 'settlement' is used both to indicate the coming of a people into the area and also the foundation and form of habitations, such as the shape of a village.
12. West, R.G., *op. cit.*, Table 12; Darby, H.C. *op. cit.*, p.3.
13. Dodgson, J. McNeil, *The Place-Names of Cheshire, Part Two*, p.26.
14. Higham, N.J., *The Origins of Cheshire*, p.31. Kenyon, D., *The Origins of Lancashire*, p.39, warns against rigidly accepting rivers as boundaries and suggests the possibility of a Brigantian group straddling the Mersey into north east Cheshire. See also Nevell, M., 1992, for this line of argument. Jones, G.B.D., in *Roman Manchester*, states the Brigantian state lasted only to AD69.
15. Ross, A., *Pagan Celtic Britain*, 1967, p.94. Kenyon, D., *op. cit.*, considers it possible that settlements of a small Celtic (British) kingdom existed north of the Mersey, and Higham, N.J., suggests a similar possibility south of the river. Also see Faulkner, P., *Flashback*, Figure 70.
16. The fort occupied 2.5-3.5 acres, Bryant, S., Morris, M., and Walker, J.S.T., *Roman Manchester*, p.11, and see Jones, G.B.D., *Roman Manchester*.
17. SMR, 363.2.
18. Ibid, 7921.
19. Information from Dr. Mike Nevell, UMAU.
20. Or might have been hidden deliberately, or lost on route.
21. Richardson, A., 'Further Evidence of Centuriation at Manchester', *Manchester Geographer*, Vol. 7, p.44.

4 TRAFFORD IN THE DARK AGES

22. Kenyon, D., *op. cit.*, p.60.

23. Kenyon, D., p.69. Bryant, S., *et al*, p.7, suggests there were a number of petty kingdoms in the north-west with a mixture of Roman and native traits.

24. Mills, D., *The Place-Names of Lancashire*, p.81 and Eckwall, E., *The Place-Names of Lancashire*.

25. Dodgson, *op. cit.*, *Part One*, considers the last element of Bollin to be pre-Saxon, perhaps related to the Celtic 'hlynn', or 'fast flowing' and that the Mersey might have had the Celtic name of 'Tame'.

26. Shirley-Price, L., *Bede – A History of the English Church and People*, p.103.

27. Dodgson, J. McNeil, 'The English Arrival in Cheshire', *Transactions of the Historic Society of Lancashire and Cheshire*, Vol. 119, 1967, p.35. Dodgson suggests peaceful infiltration along Roman roads. This gives some credibility to the claim that the road from Hale to Dunham was Roman because its presence may have assisted ingress and the foundation of Anglo-Saxon settlements along it.

28. Morgan, P., ed., *Domesday Book; Cheshire*, p.270a and last map.

29. GMAU, *Nico Ditch (Carr Ditch) Winchester Road, Urmston – An Archaeological Evaluation*.

30. Dodgson, *The Place-Names of Cheshire, Part Two*, p.34. Bryant, *et al*, p.11, suggest the forts at Warburton and Manchester might have reflected the importance of this area as a focal point between north Wales, Northumbria and Mercia. However, the identification of Weardbyrig with Warburton is a subject of contention.

31. Kenyon, D., p.129, Mills, p.42. Ekwall, E., states there was 'plenty of unused land to be had'. Crossland, A., *Looking Back at Urmston*, suggests 'Urmston' is derived from the personal name 'Orme' to whom Albert de Grelley, lord of Manchester, gave one carucate of land in the reign of John, 1199-1216.

32. Higham, N.J., p.164; Dodgson, *The Place-Names of Cheshire, Part Two*, p.8. Kenyon, D., 'Notes on English Place-Names 2', *Journal of the English Place-Name Society*, 21, p.25, argues that 'ing', 'ingham' and topographical names such as 'dun' were possibly founded before AD650-700, and that 'ton' and 'leah' were after 800.

33. Higham, N.J., p.164.

34. Kenyon, D., *Origins of Lancashire*, p.89.

35. Mills also suggests a possible Celtic origin for Lostock – 'beaver stream'. Dodgson, 'The English Arrival in Cheshire', p.241, states that 'wick' is a derivation from the Roman 'vicus' or civil settlement. Whittleswick was close to the site of Mamucium.

36. Dodgson, *The Place-Names of Cheshire, Part Two*, p.31, traditionally accepted. However, Pryor, H., *Looking Back at Timperley*, 1993, suggests a derivation from stone quarrying. There is a carbon dating of AD840 at Timperley Old Hall site, Derek Pierce of STAG.

37. Dodgson, *The Place-Names of Cheshire, Part Two*, see individual place-names in Bucklow Hundred. For north Trafford see Mills, *op. cit.*

38. **Fig. 4** sites and finds compiled from SMR. The Great Stone (A/S cross) and the cross at St Matthew's, Stretford, have not been shown. Place-names from Dodgson (Cheshire), Mills (Lancashire).

39. Dore, R.N., *A History of Hale, Cheshire*, pp.12 and 15.

40. At Green Head (Pryor, H., *op.cit.*, 'Introduction').

41. Swain, N.V., *A History of Sale*, p.22, and see his copy of Burdett's map, p.34.

42. Kenyon, D., *Origins of Lancashire*, pp.106-107.

43. Harris, B.E, and Thacker, A.T., *The Victoria History of the County of Chester* (VCH, Cheshire), Vol. II, p.237. For shiring see Stenton, F.M., *Anglo-Saxon England*, pp.292 and 337.

5 NORMAN TIMES

44. Husain, B.M.C., *Cheshire under the Norman Earls*, p.3.

45. Morgan, P., *op. cit.*

46. Or Hugh d'Avranches. According to Husain, B.M.C., *op. cit.*, p.3, William called Hugh from Avranches for the post after the first Earl of Chester left office.

47. Ibid, Fig. 2, p.10. See also Sharman, I., 'The De Masci Baronage' in Bayliss, D. G., ed., *Altrincham, a History*, p.20.

48. Morgan, P., section 9:17.

49. Swarbrick, J., 'Dunham Massey Hall', *Transactions of the Lancashire and Cheshire Antiquarian Society*, Vol. xlii, p.60, considers Dunham may have been altered from a timber castle to a stone shell keep, demolished before the Elizabethan period.

50. Dore, R.N., *op. cit.*, pp.20 and 146, believes 'Ullerwude' castle in east Hale was used in the rising of 1173 against Henry II. SMR Report, p.36, suggests Watch Hill castle was probably built at that time.

51. Dent, J.S., 'Recent Excavations on the Site of Stockport Castle', *Transactions of the Lancashire and Cheshire Antiquarian Society*, Vol. 79.

52. Morgan, P., *op. cit.*, inside back cover.

53. For example, Dunham, Bowdon, Hale, 1 hide each; Warburton, two half-hides.

54. Another resource was salt but though there were brine springs at Dunham Woodhouses and Bowdon used in later centuries, it is not known if these were used in the middle ages, information from John Hodgson, Rylands Library.

6 FROM NORMAN TIMES TO 1500

55. Booth, P., *The Financial Administration of the Lordship and County of Chester, 1272-1377*, Chetham Society, Vol. 28, p.2, "there can be little doubt that the county experienced considerable growth of population... between 1086 and 1349...".

56. Farrar, W., and Brownbill, J., eds., *VCH Lancaster*, Vol. V, p.46, Note 77.

57. 'Services due to the King in his Welsh Wars, Ed.I', handwritten translation of a manuscript, 20th February, 1865, author unknown; unauthenticated, Rylands Library. A knight's fee was the service to the Crown, for forty days, of a knight and his servants; this could be commuted to a money payment.

58. Dore, R.N., *op. cit.*, p.146, Fig. 6. Ullerwood, Castle Mill, Etrop Green and Ringway were in medieval Hale but not in modern Trafford. See also SMR Report, p.107.

59. In 1348-49 the Black Death had a devastating effect. See Bayliss, D.G., 'Altrincham in the Survey and Rental of Dunham Massey, 1348-49', Parts I and II, *Altrincham History Society Journals*, No.3, June 1992 and No.4, December 1992. Document reference in Rylands library – EGR 2/1/1/1. For the position in 1500, see, by the same author, 'Altrincham in Decline?', *Altrincham History Society Journal*, No.6, November 1993, p.9.

60. Kenyon, D., *Origins of Lancashire*, p.159.

61. In 1215 Ranulf III de Blunderville, Earl of Chester possessed the Honour of Lancaster. See Husain, B.M.C., p.93, and Kenyon, D., pp.167 and 175.

62. Ormerod, G., *A History of the County Palatinate and City of Chester*, Vol. I, p.531.

63. SMR computer list refers to several places as medieval 'villages' but in fact only a handful appear to have been of any size with a church or hall: Ashton, Bowdon, Dunham, Hale and Stretford. Additional settlements have been inserted such as Davyhulme, Sinderland and Ashton Woodhouses, believed to be in existence as hamlets. The precise sites of the mills at Stretford, Urmston and Flixton are not known. Sale inhabitants seem to have used mills at Ashton. Carrington and Partington mills and those on the Bollin are from SMR, Burdett's map of 1777 and from documentary evidence.

64. Peel Causeway, a road and former district in Hale, may refer to a palisade, according to Dodgson, J. McNeil, *Place-Names, Part Two*, p.24, though Dore says the name came from a nearby farm (Dore, R.N., p.6). Timperley Old Hall was surrounded by a moat and palisade, STAG, *Browsings*, October 1995.

65. The deer are one of the attractions of Dunham Park today.

66. The land surrounding Warburton Park Farm, site of the former hall, is enclosed by an embankment.

67. For identification of Sunderland Park (east of Altrincham) see GMAC, *Davenport Green, An Archaeological Assessment*, p.5. There has been some confusion of Sunderland in Hale township with Sinderland, a heath west of Altrincham. In the Altrincham borough charter of 1290, Hamon de Massey V stated that Sinderland could be used by the burgesses for cattle and pig grazing for the moment but "We shall have power at our will to fence in the aforesaid Sinderland without the contradiction of any persons" (translation by Dr. Peter McNiven of Rylands Library). In GMAC *Davenport Green, an Archaeological Assessment* (p.6) Sinderland has been transcribed as 'Sunderland' which is debateable.

68. Trafford Old Hall was immediately east of the Chester road near Brooks Bar and the old park was probably on the west side of that road.

69. For example, the Townfield ('tun' or farmstead field) at Altrincham (which field existed possibly before AD1290); also at Warburton; at Dumplington the field-name Dumplington Field contains the tun-field element. The presence of a Tom ('Town-') Field between Ross Mill and Hale Barns gives some support for the notion that Hale Barns was medieval Hale, though Dore does not support this and suggests it was more to the west near Hale Low.

70. Baguley was a manor shared by the de Masseys with two other lords in 1086; and see Ormerod, G., Vol. I, p.550.

71. Altrincham charter, 1290, Trafford Borough Council. The charter is explicit about pig keeping. Bayliss, D.G., 'Altrincham in the Survey and Rental of the Manor of Dunham Massey, AD 1348-49: Part I', *Altrincham History Society Journal*, No.3, June 1992, p.8.

72. Cox, M., Kemp, P., and Trenbath, R., *Bowdon Hall and its People*, p.5.

73. Langton, D.H., *A History of the Parish of Flixton*, p.14.

74. Morgan, P., *op. cit.*, Hale entry, 13:4.

75. Salford Hundred included places north of the Mersey in Trafford. Flixton, for example, one of Salford's manors, was in the lower baileywick of Manchester (Langton, D.H., p.13). Barton manor extended from Lancashire across the Irwell to include Old Trafford, Davyhulme, Dumplington, Bromyhurst, Whittleswick, Croft and Lostock. By 1282 it was in the hands of the Grelleys of Manchester (Farrar, W., and Brownbill, J., eds., *op. cit.*, p.366). Barton mills were in the Trafford part of Barton, by Barton Bridge and in 1282 were worth 45s.

76. Riddings Hall (riddings – 'clearings') may date from 1475. See family tree in Ormerod, Vol. I, pp.546-548. At this date Timperley moss was taken out of common and divided between three local lords and it is assumed this was for the purpose of enclosure. In mossland areas such as around Urmston drainage ditches were used as medieval boundaries as was the Carr Ditch. SMR Report, p.121.

The estimates of the size and shape of mosses on **Fig. 6** taken from early maps differ from the shape and extent of those on the geological survey maps for reasons stated in Note 5.

77. Court rolls in the Dunham archives at Rylands Library. Dunham halmote roll, 1403, ref. EGR 2/1/31. Both Dunham and Hale halmotes met at Altrincham. For Urmston halmote see Farrar, W., and Brownbill, J., eds., Vol. V, p.54.

78. Crofton, H.T., *A History of the Ancient Chapel of Stretford. Part III*, Chetham Society, Vol. 51, 1903, pp.192 and 199.

79. Langton, D.H., p.15 and Kenyon, D., *Origins of Lancashire*, Fig. 5.2, p.119.

80. Kenyon, D., ibid, p.174.

81. Langton, D.H., p.15. Other sources suggest AD1190.

82. Richards, R., *Old Cheshire Churches*, p.22.

83. Crofton, H.T., Part I, Chetham Society, Vol. 42, 1899, pp.48-49.

84. *VCH, Cheshire*, Vol. III, p.128; Leycester, Sir P., *Historical Antiquities of Cheshire*, 1673, p.225. At this date Bowdon parish contained Agden (one half), Ashley, Altrincham, Ashton-on-Mersey (one half), Baguley, Bollington (one half), Bowdon, Carrington, Dunham Massey, Hale, Partington and Timperley. After the Dissolution, for example, of Birkenhead, Henry created a new Bishopric of Chester in 1541 and the advowson was redirected from Bowdon to Chester. This link is not shown on the inset map because of its late date.

85. Ormerod, G., Vol. I, p.567.

86. *VCH, Cheshire*, Vol. III, p.171; Richards, R., p.339.

87. Kenyon, D., *Origins of Lancashire*, Fig. 6.1, p.143.

88. Sharman, I., in Bayliss, D.G., ed., *Altrincham, a History*, p.20.

89. Dore, R.N., Appendix 6. In the paragraph in this atlas carrying this note reference, the landlords named were not contemporaneous but spread across the period.

7 TRAFFORD'S FIRST BOROUGH

90. Sharman, I. and Bayliss, D.G., in Bayliss, D.G., ed., *Altrincham, a History*: Royal charter, p.23, borough charter, p.15. The inset map is based on Fig. 2.3, p.18, ibid.

91. Shercliff, W.H., *Manchester – A Short History of its Development*, p.5. Also Morris, M., *Medieval Manchester*, GMAU, p.25, notes places could not achieve urban status unless they had a market.

92. Dent, J.S., *op. cit.*, p.2.

93. Sharman, I., p.22, in Bayliss, D.G., ed., *Altrincham, a History*.

94. For a definitive account of burgess life see Carus-Wilson, E.M., 'The First Half-Century of the Borough of Stratford-upon-Avon', *English Historical Review*, Series 2, Vol. 18, 1965, p.46.

95. Bayliss, D.G., 'Altrincham in the Survey and Rental of Dunham Massey, 1348-49: Part I', *Altrincham History Society Journal*, June 1992, p.10. At the time of the Black Death seven burgesses were women holding a quarter of the number of burgages.

96. See, for example, Rigby, S.H., 'Sore Decay and Fair Dwellings: Boston and Urban Decline in the Later Middle Ages', *Midland History*, Vol. X, 1985, p.47, and Bayliss, D.G., 'Comments on the 1667 Subsidy Roll for Altrincham', *Altrincham History Society Journal*, No.11, 1996, p.10. Leland after 1500 described Altrincham as "a pore thing with a mayre".

9 EARLY LAW AND ADMINISTRATION

97. For courts in the north see Farrar, W. and Brownbill, J., eds., *op. cit.*, Flixton, p.53, the Urmston halmote, p.54. Also pp.1 and 2 and front maps in Redford, A., *History of Local Government in Manchester*, Longman, Vol. 1, 1939. Stretford was in Manchester parish. Urmston and Flixton were part held by military tenure from Manchester. Barton, which included parts of north Trafford, was also in Manchester demesne and subject to its courts.

For courts in south Trafford apart from Warburton, see Higginbottom, R.G., 'The Court Leet', in Bayliss, D.G, *Altrincham, a History*, p.39.

98. View of Frankpledge and Court Leet Rolls of the manor of Dunham in Rylands Library, Rylands ref. EGR 2/6/1. The Dunham Courts Leet and Baron at Altrincham served the area south of the Mersey apart from Warburton. See Ormerod, G., Vol. I, p.573. The View of Frankpledge regulated the system by which an inhabitant in Anglo-Saxon times was responsible for the good behaviour of ten or twelve households.

99. Of the ten cases before the Dunham Court Leet of May, 1653, one was for 'makinge a bludwipe' on someone, and four were for harbouring 'inmatts' (inmates or vagrants): Bayliss, D.G., 'A Dunham Massey Estate Court Roll for Altrincham Borough, May, 1653', *Altrincham History Society Journal*, No. 2, 1991. Altrincham workhouse, see Nickson, C., *Bygone Altrincham*, p.248.

10 TRAFFORD FROM THE SIXTEENTH TO EIGHTEENTH CENTURIES

100. See, for example, Briggs, A., *A Social History of England*, p.122 *et seq.*

101. Littler, J., *The Protector of Dunham Massey*, p.45.

102. See, for example, evidence at Bromyhurst, SMR Report, p.28. For complaints about overgrazing of the remaining commons in south Trafford area see seventeenth century Dunham court rolls, Rylands ref. 2/6/1.

103. SMR Report, p.28 and Crofton., H.T., 'Dumplington and the Holcrofts', *Transactions of the Lancashire and Cheshire Antiquarian Society*, 1906, 24, p.21.

104. Littler, *op. cit.*, p.74.

105. For Hale Chapel see Dore, R.N., p.37. With regard to St George's, Altrincham, this is not shown because it was not built until 1799 whereas the map dates from 1777.

106. Aiken, J., *A Description of the Country from Thirty to Forty miles round Manchester*, p.380.

107. Swain, N.V., *op. cit.*, p.51, *et seq.*

108. And a fortunate inheritance by the 2nd Earl of Warrington (Littler, pp.7 and 31).

109. The term 'new' Trafford Hall is only used in this atlas to distinguish the Whitleswick residence, occupied in 1720, from the 'old hall' at Old Trafford.

110. **Fig. 10** is from Yates's map of Lancashire, 1786 and Burdett's of Cheshire 1777 which are approximately the same scale but differ in detail shown. For details of early navigations see Gray, T., *A Hundred Years of the Manchester Ship Canal*, p.13.

111. Crofton, H.T., *op. cit.*, p.175.

112. SMR Report, p.81.

113. They are not shown on Burdett's map of 1777.

114. SMR Report.

115. Dunham Court Rolls, Rylands, ref. EGR 2/6/1; for Urmston, see Lawson, R., *History of Flixton*, Lawson, p.96.

116. Aiken, p.425.

117. Pryor, H., 'Local Salt Workings in the Seventeenth Century' and Trenbath, R., 'Thomas Walton, Gent.' in *The Bowdon Sheaf*, No. 8, 1986, and 'The Dunham Estate' in *The Bowdon Sheaf*, No. 25, 1995 (map).

118. Mullineux, F., *The Duke of Bridgewater's Canal*, and Dunham archives, Rylands, ref. EGR 3/7/2..

119. Dore, R.N., 'Manchester's Discovery of Cheshire', *Transactions of the Lancashire and Cheshire Antiquarian Society*, Vol. 82, 1983, p.5.

120. Bayliss, D.G., ed., *Altrincham, a History*, p.35.

11 WARBURTON IN 1757

121. Part of a map of 1757 of Sir Peter Warburton's estate at Warburton, permission of Charles Foster, Esq., Arley Hall. The map was redrawn by hand for clarity and annotated.

12 ALTRINCHAM TOWNSHIP AND TOWN IN 1799

122. Dunham archives, Rylands Library, ref. EGR 11/5/11. For **Fig. 12** there is no schedule to give an accurate percentage.

123. Aiken, p.425.

124. Census, 1801, Cheshire, Bucklow Hundred.

125. Several of these in the extreme north-east were intakes from Timperley Moss.

126. Groves, J., *Piggins, Husslements and Desperate Debts*, Chapter 2, p.36 and, same author, 'Houses in North-east Cheshire in the Period of the Great Rebuilding, 1600-1760', *Cheshire History*, 25, pp.30-39. Hodson, J.H., *Cheshire 1660-1780: Restoration to Industrial Revolution*, p.72, proposes another rebuilding in the late eighteenth century.

127. **Fig. 12**, Rylands ref. EGR 11/5/11. The town map, **Fig 12a**, is an enlarged central part of the township map. Burgages were identified from the 1838 tithe map and 1851 Board of Health survey, Altrincham library. See *Altrincham in 1799*, Altrincham History Society, Occasional Paper No.4.

13 DISCOVERING A LOST PARK AT OLD TRAFFORD

128. Higham, N.J., 'Tatton, Settlement and Land-Use in one Cheshire Township, c.AD1000-1400', *The Manchester Geographer*, Vol. 7, 1986, p.2.

129. Atkin. M.A., 'Stock Tracks along Township Boundaries', *Journal of the English Place-Name Society*, 15, 1982-83, p.27. Atkin, p.24, suggested there would be funnel-shaped driveways, sometimes called 'leaches' leading into the 'ovals'. One or two examples of this field-name and shape occur in the Trafford area. Field names in Trafford 'ovals' include Barn Field, Meadow, Rough, Hey (enclosure), Dam Croft and Horselow. Lawson, in *A History of Flixton*, mentions Great and White Leach fields. **Fig. 13** is from A Survey with Maps of the townships of Barton, Stretford, Hough, Chorley and Morley belonging to John Trafford, Esquire, 1782, Salford Local History Library. It has been touched-up for clarity and the dots added. Other oval-shaped areas include Whittleswick Hall Park (around new Trafford Hall), Dunham, Warburton and Sunderland Parks. For Old Trafford Hall see Walker, J.S.F., and Tindall, A.S., *Country Houses of Greater Manchester*, p.178.

130. Atkin, *op. cit.*, p.183 and Higham, M.C., 'The 'erg' Place-Names of Northern England', *Journal of the English Place-Name Society*, 10, 1978, pp.7-17, who notes that highly organised stock leasing operated from Celtic and Roman times. The suggestion in this atlas is that such open areas were appropriate to be sites for the caputs of invaders such as the Anglo-Saxons and Normans, and usable later for parks.

14 TOWNSHIPS OF TRAFFORD UP TO 1800

131. It has been assumed the township boundaries have been long-standing. They are taken from tithe maps of the pre-mid nineteenth century and administrative areas shown on O.S. maps of the 1920s. The settlements shown are mainly from Yates-Burdett late eighteenth century maps, SMR computer printout, Arley archive, Ormerod, Langton, Swain and Dore. It is assumed Stretford was a town (1477 persons) at this date, as well as Altrincham (1692 persons). The circles simply indicate the sites, not the sizes, of towns, villages and hamlets. Not all the dots on the map were farms, a few were private houses, inns and schools, two were workhouses. The following features from the SMR Update computer list are not included on the map: walls, aqueducts, bridges, barns (unless indicating a farm site), ice houses, dovecotes, brickyards, fields, unidentified remains, groups of cottages, town houses, the outbuildings of places (for example, at Dunham). The total distribution of churches, chapels and schools is not shown. An attempt has been made to omit sites dating from the nineteenth century. Judging from the 1757 map of Warburton, many farms shown in the nineteenth century tithe maps (1830s-40s) were in existence in the period considered in this section but without clear proof it was felt incorrect to show such farms in the tithe maps, so the farm distribution is, without doubt, understated. Some sites in eastern old Hale township have been omitted because places such as the hamlet of Ringway did not become part of Trafford. The acreages of the townships in the text are from the 1801-1851 census volumes.

15 TWO GENTLEMEN'S SEATS

133. Farrar, W., and Brownbill, J., eds., *VCH Lancashire*, Vol. IV, p.330. It is interesting to note the date of the move from the cramped Old Trafford site approximately coincided with rebuilding at Dunham Hall. Was it an attempt to keep up

with the Booths? **Fig. 15a** from the map of the estates of John Trafford, 1782.

134. Information from Bill Ashton. Inset map of Trafford Park and Hall from 1:2500 Lancashire Sheet CIII 12, rev., 1937. Also see Hayes, C., *This was Trafford Park*, p.3.

135. Details from The National Trust, *Dunham Massey*; SMR Report, p.51; Trafford MBC List of Buildings of Special Architectural or Historic Interest, 1990. **Fig. 15b** is an extract from the Dunham Massey tithe map of 1841.

136. Littler, *op. cit.*, p.75. There is no evidence of such a policy at Trafford Hall.

16 TRAFFORD IN 1801

137. **Fig. 16** from census data for townships, 1801. Occupations were listed for the three categories shown. As far as possible census data for later fifty year periods is shown in the same categories for comparison, but for male working populations only (there are problems with the 1801 data – see text). The circles are proportionate in area to the total township population, not just that of the chief place.

138. Though carrier services and professional, educational, surgical and personal services are mentioned in directories, the bulk of the entries refer to 'manufacture, trade and handicrafts'. See Hardman, J., *A Study of Altrincham and its families in 1801 and 1851*, p.16. Possibly if retailing was not considered a trade, this might account for some of the unstated 'other' activities, but the main numbers were women and children.

17 FEATURES OF THE RURAL LANDSCAPE BEFORE THE INDUSTRIAL PERIOD

139. Atkin, M.A., 'Stock Tracks along Township Boundaries', *Journal of the English Place-Name Society*, 15, p.24. The Partington 'green', Hall Croft, is illustrated by **Fig. 18j**. Partington, 1:10560 Cheshire VIII, 8 11 (1908).

140. Bayliss, D.G., ed., *Altrincham, a History*, p.15.

141. Higham, M.C., *op. cit*, p.30; Dodgson, J. McNeil, *The Place-Names of Cheshire, Part Two*, p.31.

142. GMAC, *Davenport Green*. For location of Sunderland Park see Note 67 above.

143. Cox, M., *et al*, *op. cit.*, p.3.

144. Ormerod, G., Vol. I, pp.558 and 559. With regard to halls, they are difficult to define. Conventionally halls had a history of continuous development from the wooden great halls of Dark Age chieftains, with separate outbuildings, surrounded by a stockade or other defence. It may be the frequency of small halls in south Lancashire and Cheshire reflects the former presence of a Celtic system of small landholdings through partible inheritance (gavelkind). Halls reached their greatest development from Tudor times to the Georgian period by which time many of the functions of the outbuildings had been absorbed into one building. While most early halls were the centres of manors, some later ones were the result of a landlord's great wealth. In recent times some hall-names were pretentious and a large residence or farm could be bigger than a local 'hall'. For local complexities see Walker, J.S.F., and Tindall, A.S., *op. cit.*, p.18 and Groves, J., *Piggins, Husslements and Desperate Debts*, p.7.

145. Ormerod, G., Vol. I, p.547 and SMR Report, p.107.

146. Part of the grounds of Oldfield Hall in Altrincham was called Pig Field in the

tithe schedule of 1835. This 9 acre patch might have been added to Altrincham when it was created a borough in AD1290. Pig rearing seems to have been an important task.

147. Nickson, *op. cit.*, p.253, suggests Oldfield Hall was built as a dower house by the second Earl of Warrington in the eighteenth century.

148. Bayliss, D.G., 'Altrincham in the Survey and Rental of Dunham...', *op. cit.*

149. With regard to Sir Thomas Danyers owning 120 acres in Hale, this was equivalent to the old hide at which the whole of Hale was assessed in 1086. Therefore for this holding and all the other halls and their lands to exist in the fourteenth century the cultivable area of Hale must have increased tremendously. Information about the halls is from R.N. Dore who questions the antiquity of Hale Hall. He states it was built in 1808 (*A History of Hale*, p.70) and a 'Manor House' was also built in the nineteenth century, p.78. Hale Hall, listed in SMR might have been at Hale Low, home of a branch of the Leicester family.

150. Details of most of the halls, moated and otherwise can be found in Walker, J.S.F., and Tindall, A.S., *op. cit.*, pp.63 and 174. For Timperley moat see Faulkner, P., 'Excavations at Timperley Moat', *Archaeology North West*, Vol. 7, p.16. A county map of 1828 by Swift and Hutchinson, shows Sale New Hall, Ashton New Hall, Ringway Hall and Wainman's Hall (also known as Siddall's Hall or Woodheys Hall); the last two are considered to be farms, and are not shown on **Fig. 17**, Buck Hall, in old Hale but not in modern Trafford, is not shown. The site of Ashton Old Hall on the 1828 map has been used here rather than the grid reference site in the SMR. Trafford Old Hall was two miles from Stretford. There is no evidence to suggest a place on the site of the nearby ?nineteenth century Longford Hall was the hall of the lord of Stretford. Moated sites were sometimes used as hunting lodges, GMAC Davenport Green, p.6. Daughter hamlets: Warburton – Moss Brow hamlet; Bowdon – Bow Green; Ashton – Ashton Woodhouses. On **Fig. 17** Hale Barns Green and 'Hale Green' are distinct. The latter may refer to the Well Green. Partington Hall Croft and Sale Green may have been 'normal' village greens. A park is shown at Whittleswick where one existed before it became Trafford (New) Park in 1720.

151. 1801 George John Legh estate map (TLSC). Regarding Timperley, Four Lane Ends might have originated as a village quarrying Keuper sandstone from a localised outcrop. The two hotels nearby are the Quarry Bank Hotel and the Stonemason's Arms. For details of enclosure of Hale Moss see Nickson, p.117 *et seq.*, and Bamford, F.W., *The Making of Altrincham, 1850 to 1991*, pp.42 and 59. For Carrington Moss see North West Wetlands Survey, p.73.

152. See notes 102 and 103, also Kemp, P., 'The 1654 Church Lands Survey', *The Bowdon Sheaf*, No.14, 1989 for openfield in Bowdon in the seventeenth century. Manson, S., *A History of Stretford*, found openfield operating in 1704 and commoning of animals in 1725.

18 TYPES OF SETTLEMENTS BEFORE THE MID-NINETEENTH CENTURY

153. The idea that places can 'evolve' is a traditional French geographical approach which implied a Darwinian point of view in which settlement site and change were closely related to, and could be conditioned 'deterministically' by, the environment. The approach does not stress human decision-making. Settlement spacing is a relatively recent mathematical approach which sees places as part of a geometrical matrix or pattern, with central places at the focus of a hexagonal or circular pattern and less important places further away. The shape of places may depend not only on the environment but on the culture of the people inhabiting the area and human decisions.

154. Bayliss, D.G., 'Altrincham in Decline?', *Altrincham History Society Journal*, No.6, p.9. See note 59 above.

155. **Fig. 18a** is adapted from a map based on the 1842 tithe map in Dore, R.N., *op. cit.*, p.77. The farms and other buildings on Dore's map have been represented as dots to create a pattern. Seven halls are shown, most from R.N. Dore but, as above, he contends the early existence of Hale Hall, here plotted from grid references in Walker, J.S.F., and Tindall, A.S., Vol. 2, 1985.

The series of maps in **Fig. 18** from the late eighteenth, early nineteenth century (tithe) and a few later ordnance maps shows examples of settlement patterns (in this case meaning the shape and constituents of places) in the Trafford area before the railways came, though for clarity one or two are, in fact, post-railway. All are reduced from their true scale.

156. Information from Derek Pierce.

157. **Fig. 18b** from the Timperley tithe map, 1835. Pryor, H., *op. cit.*, suggests Green Head was the ancient centre of Timperley. SMR identifies medieval Timperley in its present location (called Timperley in Swires and Hutchinson 1828 map and Four Lane Ends in the 1835 tithe). See note 151.

158. **Fig. 18c** Carrington from O.S. 1:2,500 1876, differing little from the 1838 tithe map but selected because it is clearer.

159. **Fig. 18d**, Riddings, redrawn for clarity from the Timperley tithe map of 1835. Note north is to bottom left. See Faulkner, P., *Flashback*, p.91.

160. **Fig. 18e** redrawn from the Bowdon tithe map, 1838.

161. **Fig. 18f** from the Urmston 1:10,560 Lancashire Sheet 110 of 1848.

162. **Fig. 18g** redrawn from the Ashton-on-Mersey tithe map of 1845.

163. **Fig. 18h** Stretford from the Trafford estates map of 1782 reproduced on computer for clarity.

164. **Fig. 18i** Dumplington and Whittleswick from the Trafford estates map of 1782.

165. **Fig. 18j** Partington from the O.S. 1:2,500, 1876.

166. **Fig. 18k** Millbank from the O.S. 1:2,500, 1876.

167. **Fig. 18l** Sale redrawn from a very smudged George John Legh estate map of 1801 (TLSC). For Sale in relation to New Hall and Sale Green see Newhill, J., *Sale, Cheshire, in 1841*, p.60. Swain indicates the likely site of ancient Sale to be in the Dane Road area (Swain, p.14).

19 TRAFFORD IN 1851

168. In the Altrincham Town's Minute Book for 1827 a letter from Lord Stamford voiced his objections to the profligacy of the Court Leet dinners.

169. Bamford, F.W., *Men and Mansions of Dunham Massey*, p.12.

170. In general terms the Stamfords were pro-canals and industry, the de Traffords were anti-canals and industry.

171. Bamford, F.W., *Men and Mansions of Dunham Massey*, and Kemp P., *Higher*

Downs Altrincham: A Short History, Bowdon History Society, illustrate the involvement of the Stamfords on building in south Trafford.

172. The Brooks, a family of bankers, owned much land in Sale and Timperley and gave their name to Brooklands Road and Brooks Bar. They commissioned many buildings such as Lloyds Bank in Old Market Place, Altrincham (Grade II). The Harrops were the fourth largest landowners in Hale after the Stamfords, Egertons and Fodens (Dore, R.N., p.70).

173. The Altrincham tithe map, 1835, shows housing spreading on to those strips of the former Town Field which were owned by small landlords.

174. On **Fig. 12**, the 1799 Stamford estate map of Altrincham, Rylands Library, some medieval strips north-west of the town had been divided into squarer patches for market gardening.

175. Enclosure map of Sale, 1806 (TLSC).

176. Fleming, E.R., in Bayliss, *Altrincham, a History*, p.99. For Local Board offices (after 1852) see *The Borough of Altrincham Charter Celebration booklet*, 1937, p.16. The offices were formerly a residence. For the Town Hall of 1849, see Fitzpatrick, G., *Altrincham Past and Present*, pp.10 and 11. Also Morrison, B.D., *Looking Back at Altrincham*, p.11.

177. **Fig. 19** from census data, 1851. Total populations are given for townships as in 1801, but occupations are for whole Registration Districts only for males over twenty years in well over a hundred sub-categories, here resolved into five. The Trafford area fell into two districts – Altrincham, Area 454 and Barton-on-Irwell, Area 476.

178. Don Bayliss, Hilda Bayliss, Chris Hill, Judith Lipman and Hazel Pryor, *Altrincham in 1841*, pp.48-49.

20 THE MID-NINETEENTH CENTURY

179. **Fig. 20** has been compiled from two county sheets, the south sheet of 1848 and the north sheet of the 1880s hence the abrupt ending of the Urmston railway line! The highland was shown by hachures of which there were only a few in the Hale area and these have not reproduced.

21 TRAFFORD IN 1901

180. **Fig. 21** source – census, county Occupation Tables, 1901. It was not possible to replicate the divisions of **Figs. 16** and **19**; occupations (reduced from ten categories) are for males over ten years in C.B.s, M.B.s and U.D.s with over 5000 population – hence no details for small places. A major problem is that the categories themselves differed for each county making comparisons between north and south Trafford rather impossible. Circles are proportionate to total populations. Reference for Ship Canal – Harford, I., *Manchester and its Ship Canal Movement*, p.167. The centre for Hale had shifted from Hale Barns by this date.

Parish creation accompanied population growth in or just after the nineteenth century: Altrincham St George 1799/1812 (Nickson, *op. cit*, p.154 and Fairley, G., in Bayliss, *Altrincham a History*, p.58, give 1868); St John 1867; St Vincent de Paul 1904; Loreto Convent 1909; St Alban 1910; Ashton 1856; St Mary Magdalene 1894. Barton 1849; St Catherine 1843. Davyhulme Christchurch 1868, St Mary 1889; Dunham Massey St Margaret 1855; St Mark 1866; Hale St Peter's 1892; Old Trafford St Hilda 1899; St Cuthbert 1902; St John 1902; St Thomas 1858; Partington 1889; Sale St Anne 1856; St Paul 1884; St Joseph 1884; Stretford All Saints 1904; St Bride 1879; St Peter 1892/1906; Urmston St Clement 1868; Warburton (new church) 1869. There were several ancient parishes remaining, some in part: Baguley, Bowdon, Carrington (1759), Warburton, Flixton (1190, registers from 1570), Ringway, Stretford (registers from 1598). Sources: Youngs, F.A., *Guide to the Local Administrative Units of England*, Vol. II, Royal Historical Society, 1991, Lancashire. pp.139-215; Cheshire 3-43. Registers – Hewitt, K.N. and Boxall, F.A., *List of Heraldic and Genealogical Sources*, Kent, 1962. Map for Sale area – Borough Engineer, Sale 1951. Sale Local Studies Centre 40384/16. St Catherine – Baines, E., *History of the County Palatine and Duchy of Lancashire*, 1888, Vol. I, p.263. Information also from Jayne Britton (TLSC) and from Len King for the Urmston area. For nonconformist churches and chapels, see Merrell, C.M., in Bayliss, D.G., ed., *Altrincham, a History*, p.61; Fitzpatrick, G., *Altrincham Past and Present*, pp.31 and 46; Dore, R.N., *op. cit.*, p.127; Langton, D.H., p.88-90.

181. Bamford, F.W., *Broadheath*, 1885-1895.

22 COMMUNICATIONS FROM THE EIGHTEENTH CENTURY

182. Turnpike details on **Fig. 22** from Harrison, W., 'The Development of Turnpikes in Lancashire and Cheshire', *Transactions of the Lancashire and Cheshire Antiquarian Society*, Vol. IV, 1886, p.80. See also Faulkner P., *op. cit.*, Figs. 83 and 92.

183. For information see Directories, for example, Pigot and Company, 1834; Pigot and Slater, 1841; Balshaw, C.V., *Stranger's Guide* (Altrincham area) 1858.

184. A large new warehouse was built west of Broadheath bridge in 1833. Timber, animals, vegetables, stone, corn, coal, nightsoil and textile materials passed along the canal. It is perhaps not a coincidence that Lord Stamford, with interests in the canal, on which cotton could be carried, owned the Styal land on which Quarry Bank Mill was built. O'Mahoney, C., *QBM Memoranda*, Vol. 1, QBM Trust, 1989, p.8. For details of the building of the canal see Bridgewater Canal documents, EGR 3/7/2, Dunham archives, Rylands Library, note 118 above, and Malet, H., *Bridgewater, The Canal Duke, 1736-1803*. Stretford in the nineteenth century was noted for its pig markets. The pigs were reputedly brought by canal, and earned the town the nickname 'Porkhampton'.

185. The poor condition of the present road and the narrow paths which represent the former alignment suggest there had not been a major road between Broadheath and Highgate in recent centuries.

186. Barton was an ancient bridge site. No bridge was shown on mid-nineteenth century maps at Warburton, where Hollins Ferry was the crossing point. Tolls are still levied to cross a bridge at Warburton over the Mersey pre-dating the adjacent iron Manchester Ship Canal bridge, though the course of the Mersey is now dry beneath the old bridge! The tolls are not for crossing the MSC bridge – information from Bill Ashton. With reference to the building of the MSC and personalities involved see Leech, Sir T. Bosdin, *History of the Manchester Ship Canal*; Owen, D., *The Manchester Ship Canal*; Gray, T., *A Hundred Years of the Manchester Ship Canal*, and Bayliss, D.G., 'Marshall Stevens', *Altrincham History Journal*, No.8, September, 1993, p.8.

187. I am indebted to Andrew Macfarlane for supplying almost all the information

regarding railways. See also Macfarlane in Bayliss, D.G., ed., *Altrincham, a History*, pp.88-92. For Trafford Park railways see Thorpe, D., *The Railways of the Manchester Ship Canal*, p.77. For early commuting travel see Dore, R.N., 'Manchester's Discovery of Cheshire', *Transactions of the Lancashire and Cheshire Antiquarian Society*, Vol. 82, 1983, pp.3-5, note 119 above.

23 INDUSTRIALISATION

188. Fig. 23a, Broadheath from 1:2500 Cheshire Sheet XVII.6, 1910.

Sources for Broadheath: Sparkes, C.A., in Bayliss, D.G., ed., *Altrincham, a History*, p.120; Bamford, F.W., *Broadheath, 1885-1895* and *The Making of Altrincham 1850-91*, p.60.

189. Fig. 23b from Trafford Local Studies Centre. Sir Humphrey de Trafford was reluctant to sell Trafford Park for industrial purposes – Hayes, C., *This was Trafford Park*, p.3. For a full history see Nicholls, R., *A Hundred Years of Trafford Park*.

190. Trafford Official Guide, 1994, p.49.

191. Information from Ian Sandham.

192. From the 1:25000 Sheet SJ79, 1975, with permission from the Ordnance Survey.

24 LOCAL GOVERNMENT

193. Report on the Borough of Altrincham, Reports from the Commissioners (George Hutton Wilkinson), 1834.

194. Joan French in Bayliss, D.G., ed., *Altrincham, a History*, p.47.

195. **Fig. 24** compiled from O.S admin. maps, 1:126720 of Lancashire and Cheshire, 1928, SMR Report, and Cross, A.N., *A Select Gazetteer of Local Government Areas for Greater Manchester Council*.

25 THE EARLY TWENTIES

196. **Fig. 25** reduced from O.S.1:63360, 1924 with extra names for clarity.

26 AT THE END OF WORLD WAR II

197. **Fig. 26** reduced from O.S. 1:63360, Sheet 101, 1947 with additions.

27 TRAFFORD IN 1951

198. **Fig. 27** 1951 figures – census county volumes; circles show total populations and data from the Industry Tables, orders and selected units and status aggregates for occupied males aged fifteen and over, covering the M.B.s, U.D.s and (totals for the whole of) R.D.s, twenty-four main categories with sub-divisions, here summarised into three.

28 CHANGES IN PLANNING STYLES; SPORTS AREAS; TYPES OF GROWTH

199. **Fig. 28a** Gorsehill from 1:2500 Lancashire Sheet CIV13, 1931.

200. **Fig. 28b** Stretford, from 1:2500 Lancashire Sheet CV13, 1910.

201. **Fig. 28c** Trafford Park centre from 1:2500 Lancashire Sheet CIII16, rev. 1937.

202. **Fig. 28d** Oldfield Brow from 1:10560 Cheshire Sheet XVIII, 1938.

203. **Fig. 28e** Davyhulme from 1:2500 Lancashire Sheet CX2, 1928.

204. **Fig. 28f** Upper Altrincham from 1:2500 Cheshire Sheet XVIII6, 1910.

205. **Fig. 28g** Sale from 1:2500 Cheshire Sheet IX11, 1910.

206. **Fig. 28h** Hale Barns from 1:2500 Sheet SJ 7886-SJ 7986.

207. **Fig. 28i** Old Trafford flats from 1:10000 Sheet SJ 78 NE.

208. **Fig. 28j** Old Trafford sports areas from 1:2500 Lancashire Sheet CV13, 1931.

209. **Fig. 29k** Flixton from 1:2500 Lancashire Sheet CX2, 1928.

210. **Fig. 28l** Urmston from 1:2500 Lancashire Sheet CX3, 1937.

211. **Fig. 28m** Altrincham and Hale from 1:10560, 1910, Sheet XVIII NW. The empty building blocks were built between 1907 and 1938.

For a description of New Street, Chapel Street and Newtown, see Fitzpatrick, G., in Bayliss, D.G., ed., *Altrincham, a History*, pp.93-94, and Bamford, F.W., *The Making of Altrincham*, p.32 et seq.

29 RECENT TIMES

212. **Fig. 29** from O.S.1:50,000 Landranger Sheet 109 reduced with permission from the Ordnance Survey. Population figures from Trafford MBC. As noted, the map goes beyond the boundary of Trafford in the south and includes Manchester Airport, not in Trafford. There have been minor adjustments of boundary round Trafford (for example, in Brooklands) but not on the scale to include the airport! I am grateful to George Morton, Bill Ashton and Frank Prest for information for this section.

213. See Stocks, N.R., in Bayliss, D.G., ed., *Altrincham, a History*, p.133, especially the map.

214. Differences from 1:50000 maps of the 1980s reflect the run-down of both Trafford Park and Carrington because fewer buildings are shown at these places on the most recent edition, for example, the sites of GEC and the park village are shown partially cleared. The new road systems in the Park and at Old Trafford are not shown, nor the Dumplington site though part of this is open to trade. Broadheath railway bridge over the A56 has now gone. Sale Grammar School for Boys is still shown on Moss Lane, its former site in Sale, though this is now covered by houses.

30 TRAFFORD IN THE FUTURE

215. **Fig. 30** condensed and generalised from two 1:10000 maps accompanying the draft Unitary Development Plan, Trafford MBC, 1992.

SOURCES

PRIMARY SOURCES

MAPS

Ordnance Survey Maps
1:63360: 1848, 1885, 1924, 1947, (MUDG). 1:50000: 1995 and 1:25000: 1957 with O.S. permission.
O.S Admin. maps, 1:126720 of Lancashire and Cheshire, 1928 (MUDG).
1:2500, 1:10000 and 1:10560 for settlement plans of Altrincham, Broadheath, Carrington, Davyhulme, Flixton, Hale Barns, Old Trafford, Partington, Sale, Stretford, Urmston, various years (MUDG, TLSC).
Geological Survey (Drift): Stockport and Manchester Sheets (MUDG).

Other maps
Tithe maps: Altrincham 1835, Ashton-on-Mersey 1838, Bowdon 1838, Dunham Massey 1841, Timperley 1838, (Cheshire Record Office).
Speed's maps of Lancashire and Cheshire, ex-Greater Manchester County (MUDG).
Part of a map of 1757 of Sir Peter Warburton's estate at Warburton, permission of Charles Foster, Esq. (Arley Hall).
A Survey with Maps of the townships of Barton, Stretford, Hough, Chorley and Morley belonging to John Trafford, Esquire, 1782 (Salford Local History Library).
Burdett's map of Cheshire, 1777 (MUDG).
Yates's map of Lancashire 1786 (MUDG).
Dunham estate map of Altrincham, 1799. Dunham archives, (Rylands ref. EGR 11/5/11).
1801 George John Legh estate map (TLSC).
Enclosure map of Sale, 1806. 'A plan of the common and waste lands in the Township of Sale ...' (TLSC).
Map of parishes for Sale area – Borough Engineer, Sale M.B., 1951. (TLSC).
A Cheshire county map of 1828, Swift and Hutchinson (TLSC).
1924 map of the land of the Trafford Park Company (TLSC).

MANUSCRIPT SOURCES

Rylands Library
'Services due to the King in his Welsh Wars, Ed.I', handwritten trans. ms., 1865, author unknown; unauthenticated; may be spurious. Rylands ref. EGR 2/1/1/1.
Dunham court rolls including View of Frankpledge and Court Leet, Rylands ref. EGR 2/6/1.
Dunham halmote roll, 1403. Rylands ref. EGR 2/1/31.
Bridgewater Canal: Dunham archives, Rylands, ref. EGR 3/7/2..

Trafford Local Studies Centre
1667 Poll Tax with notes on 1664 hearth tax – transcribed by Jill Groves (from originals in the Leicester-Warren Archives, Cheshire Record Office).

Altrincham Library
1851 Board of Health survey and map.
Altrincham Town's Minute Book for 1827.
Altrincham borough charter, 1290, Trafford MBC.

Manchester City Central Library
Census volumes 1801-1951

PRINTED SOURCES

Trafford Local Studies Centre
1834 Report on the Borough of Altrincham. Reports from the Commissioners (George Hutton Wilkinson).
The Borough of Altrincham Charter Celebration booklet, 1937.
Directories, for example, Pigot and Co., Cheshire, 1834; Pigot and Slater, Manchester and Salford, 1841.
Also recent population figures.

STAG
Dates of finds at Timperley Old Hall site.

TMBC
Trafford MBC, *List of Buildings of Special Architectural or Historic Interest*, 1990.
Trafford MBC, *Unitary Development Plan*, 1992.

Others
Balshaw, C., *Stranger's Guide to Altrincham*, 1858, reprinted by E.J. Morten, 1973.
Aiken, J., *A Description of the Country from Thirty to Forty miles round Manchester*, London, 1793, reprinted Kelley, New York, 1968.

SECONDARY SOURCES

BOOKS

Baines, E., *History of the County Palatine and Duchy of Lancashire*, Vols 1-5, 1888.
Bamford, F.W., *The Making of Altrincham, 1850 to 1991*, Frank Bamford, 1991.
Bamford, F.W., *Men and Mansions of Dunham Massey*, Frank Bamford, 1991.
Bamford, F.W., *Broadheath, 1885-1895: A Century of Industry*, Frank Bamford, 1995.
Bayliss, D. G., *Altrincham, a History*, Willow, 1992.
Bayliss, D.G, *Altrincham in 1799*, Occasional Paper No.4, Altrincham History Society.
Bayliss D.G., Hilda Bayliss, Chris Hill, Judith Lipman and Hazel Pryor, *Altrincham in 1841*, Occasional Paper No.5, Altrincham History Society, 1994.
Booth, P., *The Financial Administration of the Lordship and county of Chester, 1272-1377*, Chetham Society, 3rd series, Vol. 28, 1981.
Briggs, A., *A Social History of England*, Book Club Associates, 1983.
Bryant, S., Morris, M., and Walker, J.S.T., *Roman Manchester*, GMAU, 1986.

Cox, M., Kemp, P., and Trenbath R., *Bowdon Hall and its People: A study of the hall and its estate, its owners and its tenants*, Bowdon History Society, 1994.

Crofton, H.T., 'A History of the Ancient Chapel of Stretford, Part I', *Chetham Society*, Vol. 42, 1899.

Crofton, H.T., 'A History of the Ancient Chapel of Stretford, Part III', *Chetham Society*, Vol. 51, 1903,

Crossland, A., *Looking back at Urmston*, Willow, 1983.

Cross, A.N., *A Select Gazetteer of Local Government Areas for Greater Manchester Council*, GMC, 1982.

Darby, H.C., *An Historical Geography of England to 1700*, Cambridge, 1948.

Dodgson, J. McNeil, *The Place-Names of Cheshire, Parts One and Two*, CUP, 1970.

Dore, R.N., editor, *A History of Hale, Cheshire: From Domesday to Dormitory*, Sherratt, 1972.

Ekwall, E., *The Place-Names of Lancashire*, MUP, 1922.

Farrar, W., and Brownbill, J., eds., *The Victoria History of the County Palatine of Lancaster*, Vol.V, Constable, London, 1911.

Faulkner, P., *Flashback*, STAG, 1988.

Fitzpatrick, G., *Altrincham Past and Present*, Willow, 1990.

GMAC, *Davenport Green, An Archaeological Assessment*, GMAC, 1994.

GMAU, *Nico Ditch (Carr Ditch) Winchester Road, Urmston – An Archaeological Evaluation*, GMAU, 1992.

Gray, T., *A Hundred Years of the Manchester Ship Canal*, Aurora, 1994.

Groves, J., *Piggins, Husslements and Desperate Debts: A social history of North-east Cheshire through wills and probate inventories, 1600 to 1760*, Northern Writers Advisory Services, 1994.

Hall, D., Wells, C.E. and Huckerby, E., *North West Wetlands Survey, The Wetlands of Greater Manchester*, Lancaster, 1995.

Hardman, J., *A Study of Altrincham and its Families in 1801 and 1851*, Hardman, 1989.

Harford, I., *Manchester and its Ship Canal Movement*, Ryburn (Keele), 1994.

Harris, B.E, and Thacker, A.T., *The Victoria History of the County of Chester*, Vols II and III, OUP, 1987 and 1990.

Hayes, C., *This was Trafford Park*, Northern Publishing Services and Trafford MBC, 1993.

Hewitt, K.N. and Boxall, F.A., *List of Heraldic and Genealogical Sources*, Kent, 1962.

Higham, N.J., *The Origins of Cheshire*, MUP, 1993.

Hodson, J.H., *Cheshire 1660-1780: Restoration to Industrial Revolution*, Vol. 9, Cheshire Community Council, 1978.

Husain, B.M.C., *Cheshire under the Norman Earls*, Vol. 4, Cheshire Community Council, 1973.

Jones, G.B.D., *Roman Manchester*, Sherratt, 1974.

Kemp, P., *Higher Downs Altrincham: A Short History*, Bowdon History Society.

Kenyon, D., *The Origins of Lancashire*, MUP, 1991.

Langton, D.H., *A History of the Parish of Flixton*, Langton, Manchester, 1898, reprinted Trafford MBC, 1991.

Lawson, R., *A History of Flixton*, Lawson, 1898.

Leech, Sir T. Bosdin, *History of the Manchester Ship Canal*, Sherratt and Hughes, 1907.

Leech, H.J., *Tales and Sketches of Old Altrincham and Bowdon*, 1880.

Leycester, Sir P., *Historical Antiquities of Cheshire*, London, 1673.

Littler, J., *The Protector of Dunham Massey*, Joyce Littler, 1993.

Malet, H., *Bridgewater, The Canal Duke, 1736-1803*, MUP, 1977.

Masson, S., *A History of Stretford*, Sherratt, 1976.

Mills, D., *The Place-Names of Lancashire*, Batsford, 1976.

Morgan, P., ed., *Domesday Book: Cheshire*, Phillimore, 1978.

Morris, M., ed., *Medieval Manchester*, GMAU, 1983.

Morrison, B.D., *Looking Back at Altrincham*, Willow, 1980.

Mullineux, F., *The Duke of Bridgewater's Canal*, Eccles and District Historical Society, 1959.

National Trust, *Dunham Massey*, handbook, 1981.

Nevell, M, *A History and Archaeology of Tameside. Volume 1: Tameside, 1066-1700*, Tameside MBC, 1991.

Nevell, M, *A History and Archaeology of Tameside. Volume 2: Tameside Before 1066*, Tameside MBC, 1992.

Nevell, M, *A History and Archaeology of Tameside. Volume 3: Tameside 1700-1930*, Tameside MBC, 1993.

Newhill, J., *Sale, Cheshire in 1841: Its People and Their Lives*, Ashton and Sale History Society, 1994.

Nicholls, R., *A Hundred Years of Trafford Park*, Phillimore, 1996.

Nickson, C., *Bygone Altrincham*, reprinted E.J. Morten 1979.

Ormerod, G., *A History of the County Palatinate and City of Chester*, Vol.I, London, 1882.

Owen, D., *The Manchester Ship Canal*, MUP, 1983.

Pryor, H., *Looking Back at Timperley*, Willow, 1993.

Redford, A., *History of Local Government in Manchester*, Vol.1, Longmans, 1939.

Richards, R., *Old Cheshire Churches*, Batsford, 1947.

Ross, A., *Pagan Celtic Britain*, Cardinal, 1967.

Shercliff, W.H., *Manchester – A Short History of its Development*, Manchester Town Hall, 1972.

Shirley-Price, L., *Bede – A History of the English Church and People*, Penguin, 1979.

Stenton, F.M., *Anglo-Saxon England*, OUP, 1971.

Stretford Local History Society, *Stretford, People and Places 1928-1945*, Countryside Books, 1985.

Swain, N.V., *A History of Sale*, Sigma, 1988.

Sylvester, D. and Nulty, G., *The Historical Atlas of Cheshire*, Cheshire Community Council, 1958.

Walker, J.S.F., and Tindall, A.S., *Country Houses of Greater Manchester*, GMAU, 1985.

West, R.G., *Pleistocene Geology and Biology*, Longman, 2nd ed., 1977.

Youngs, F.A. *Guide to the Local Administrative Units of England*, Vol.II, Royal Historical Society, 1991.

ARTICLES

Ashton, Bill, 'The Manchester Ship Canal 1894-1994', *Stretford Chronicle*, Spring 1994.

Atkin M.A. and Higham, M.C., 'The 'erg' Place-Names of Northern England', *Journal of the English Place-Name Society*, 10, 1978.

Atkin. M.A., 'Stock Tracks along Township Boundaries', *Journal of the English Place-Name Society*, 15, 1982-83.

Bayliss, D.G., 'A Dunham Massey Estate Court Roll for Altrincham Borough, May 1653', *Altrincham History Society Journal*, No.2, 1991.

Bayliss, D.G., 'Altrincham in the Survey and Rental of Dunham Massey, 1348-49, Parts I and II', *Altrincham History Society Journals*, Nos.3 and 4, 1992.

Bayliss, D.G., 'Altrincham in Decline?' *Altrincham History Society Journal*, No.6, 1993.

Bayliss, D.G., 'Marshall Stevens', *Altrincham History Journal*, No.8, 1993.

Bayliss, D.G., 'Comments on the 1667 Subsidy Roll for Altrincham', *Altrincham History Society Journal*, No.11, 1996.

Carus-Wilson, E.M., 'The First Half-Century of the Borough of Stratford-upon-Avon', *English Historical Review*, Ser.2, Vol.18, 1965.

Crofton., H.T., 'Dumplington and the Holcrofts', *Transactions of the Lancashire and Cheshire Antiquarian Society*, Vol. 24, 1906.

Dent, J.S., 'Recent Excavations on the Site of Stockport Castle', *Transactions of the Lancashire and Cheshire Antiquarian Society*, Vol.79, 1977.

Dodgson, J. McNeil, 'The English Arrival in Cheshire', *Transactions of the Historic Society of Lancashire and Cheshire*, Vol.119, 1967.

Dore, R.N., 'Manchester's Discovery of Cheshire', *Transactions of the Lancashire and Cheshire Antiquarian Society*, Vol.82. 1983.

Faulkner, P., 'Excavations at Timperley Moat', *Archaeology North West*, Vol.7.

Groves, J., 'Houses in North-east Cheshire in the Period of the Great Rebuilding, 1600-1760', *Cheshire History*, 25.

Harrison, W., 'The Development of Turnpikes in Lancashire and Cheshire', *Transactions of the Lancashire and Cheshire Antiquarian Society*, Vol.iv, 1886.

Higham, N.J., 'Tatton, Settlement and Land-Use in one Cheshire Township, c.AD1000-1400', *The Manchester Geographer*, Vol.7, 1986.

Kemp, P., 'The 1654 Church Lands Survey', *The Bowdon Sheaf*, No.14, 1989.

Kemp, P., 'Moss Farm', *The Bowdon Sheaf*, No.17, 1991.

Kenyon, D., 'Notes on English Place-Names 2', *Journal of the English Place-Name Society*, 21, 1988.

O'Mahoney, C., *QBM Memoranda, Vol. 1*, QBM Trust, 1989.

Pryor, H., 'Local Salt Workings in the Seventeenth Century', *The Bowdon Sheaf*, No. 8, 1986.

Richardson, A., 'Further Evidence of Centuriation at Manchester', *Manchester Geographer*, Vol. 7, 1986.

Rigby, S.H., 'Sore Decay and Fair Dwellings: Boston and Urban Decline in the Later Middle Ages', *Midland History*, Vol.x, 1985.

Swarbrick, J., 'Dunham Massey Hall', *Transactions of the Lancashire and Cheshire Antiquarian Society*, Vol.xlii, 1925.

Trenbath, R., 'Thomas Walton, Gentleman', *The Bowdon Sheaf*, No.8, 1986

Trenbath, R., 'The Dunham Massey Estate', *The Bowdon Sheaf*, No.25, 1995.

INDEX

(refers to main text and notes section only, not captions)

Ullerwood, 10, 12
Unitary Development Plan, 70, 72
Urban District, 54, 58, 66
Urmston, 4, 6, 10, 12, 17, 20, 30, 35, 42, 44, 46, 48, 54, 56, 57, 58, 65, 70, 74
    Urmston Moor, 20

vagrancy, 17, 76
Vaudrey family, 36
vegetable-growing, 22, 48, 58
Venables family, 14

villages, 32, 35, 52, 60, 70, 75

Warburton, 4, 6, 8, 10, 12, 16, 17, 20, 21, 30, 32, 35, 36, 40, 42, 46, 48, 50, 54, 74, 78, 79
    Warburton St Werburgh, 12, 18, 21
    Warburton Hall, 21, 34, 44
    Warburton Moss, 20, 21, 34
    Warburton Park, 21, 32
    Warburton Priory, 14
waste, 10, 34, 35
Watch Hill Castle, Dunham Massey, 12

Watersmeet, 48
Watling Street, 2, 6, 20, 24, 26, 32, 38, 48, 50, 73, 79
Whittleswick, 8, 16, 18, 20, 28, 36, 40, 76, 78
Wilderspool, 20
Woodheys Hall, Sale, 44, 57
workhouse, 17

yeomanry, 18, 35